Forward Motion

From Bach to Bebop

A Corrective Approach to
Jazz Phrasing

By

Hal Galper

ISBN 1-883217-41-5
©2005 Sher Music Co., P.O. Box 445 Petaluma, CA 94953
www.shermusic.com

A NOTE TO THE READER

The musical examples in this book can be played on-line, inter-actively, in your browser, by going to the following URL **http://www.amenablemusic.net/fmb/examples.htm**. This is the same page from which you can access the TipSheet and *Forward Motion* FAQs. To play the examples you'll need to download a small, and nifty, freeware program, the **Myriad Music Plug-In** from the Myriad Music web site at **http://www.myriad-online.com/plugmain.htm**.

Both Windows and Mac versions are available. The Myriad Music Plug-In enables to you play, display, transpose and print files created with Harmony Assistant, directly from your web browser. The Mac version is 969K. The Windows version is 1074k. Both take only about 5 minutes to download and, if you follow the directions, are easy to install in your browser. Unlike MP3, RealAudio and WAV. files, the Myriad files are low memory and download quickly.

Hal Galper

ACKNOWLEDGMENTS

The following deserve thanks for the contributions they have offered: Dave Liebman for his Forward, Andrew Scott for his proofing and expert comments, Didier Guillion at Myriad for his patience and expertise with my ineptness with Harmony Assistant. The author accepts full responsibility for any and all mistakes, glitches and gaffs herein.

Reader comments are welcome. For contact info, please visit my web site at: **http://www.halgalper.com.**

**This book is dedicated to the fond memory of
Madame Margaret Chaloff
who opened the door to *Forward Motion*.**

TABLE OF CONTENTS

FORWARD

By Dave Liebman

Hal and myself go back to the first loft I had on west 19th Street. In fact I remember a session with Bob Moses, Randy and Mike Brecker doing some fusion stuff back in 1969. He is definitely one of the senior citizens of jazz having served his time with greats like Cannonball Adderley and Phil Woods. Hal has recorded some remarkable music, ran his own trio from top to bottom meaning music, bookings, PR et al, for most of the 1990s; authored a book on the touring musician that is a goldmine of information; been one of the prime sources of straight forward talk in the jazz education business and most important, a great pianist to have playing alongside you. It has been my pleasure many times to "hit" with Galps.

Hal is from the generation slightly ahead of mine having done his early apprenticeship years in the 60s, when there were few jazz books or courses to take part in. But like myself, Hal thought through a lot through the years about how to articulate his specific musical ideas. The material in this book has been in the works for decades with articles, pamphlets, etc., along the way explaining parts of the philosophy from time to time. I have in my collection Hal's notes from the early 80s about *Forward Motion*, pentatonics and upper structures. But alongside the desire to explain the music, he also possesses a great gift for writing in such a way that you feel like he is there in front of you giving the lesson. His language is clear, precise and thoughtful with a pervasive sense of humor throughout as well wonderful stories from the real jazz world that underscores his points.

Galps sums it up in his own words at the beginning of Chapter Three: "Improvising is the reordering of the notes of a scale into their strongest melodic possibilities." "*Forward Motion*" is chock full of ideas that most improvisers never thought of in such detail in order to achieve this "reordering", or put simply, theme and variations ad infinitum. What Hal concentrates on for the most part is the very subject that is least discussed in texts of any sort, which is the use of rhythm, jazz rhythm to be exact, in order to improvise countless ways on a given line. We are used to books of variations based on pitch changes, harmonic super-impositions, syncopation, etc., all harmonic and melodic ideas that Hal does touch upon also. But with his emphasis on the upbeat and half time as the important mechanisms for feeling jazz rhythm along with other concepts, Galper offers countless ways of manipulating both simple and more complex material for unlimited possibilities. The *Forward Motion* theory uses concepts of displacement, sequential reordering, unusual accent points, appoggiaturas strategically placed and more.

There are some ingenious ideas throughout. One in particular was very interesting: try using the rhythms only of a complicated head like "Confirmation" but in the context of another tune and chord cycle for freeing up one's patterned ways of thinking. His comments on King Oliver's admonishment to Louis Armstrong about the importance of melody before one attempts embellishment and even some insight into Bach's use of "FM" make for entertaining reading. And the truly innovative aspect of *Forward Motion* is the interactive part. Students will be able to hear and play along with the written examples. Hal is up on the techno scene for sure!

I am so pleased that someone has addressed these ideas, especially on rhythmic issues in a coherent, unified and practical manner with abundant examples to play. Even glancing at this book will generate new ideas for improvisers at any level.

David Liebman

PREFACE

"The trouble with people who do not know is that they do not know what they do not know." Gene Lees, Jan. 2001 issue: Jazzletter.

This is the umpteenth time I've started to write a jazz instruction book. Each time I'd get depressed and stop at a certain point and put it in the circular file. Four major questions stopped me in my tracks every time.

With so many jazz instruction books now on the market does the world need another one?

For many reasons the answer is yes. The general tendency of jazz education toward a unified pedagogy is not in jazz's best interests. One would be hard put to argue against a general philosophy that the more ways one looks at a subject, the more one achieves a fuller enhancement of understanding and perspective of it. One of the historically basic tenets of jazz has been the development of each musician's individual voice.

This tendency toward uniformity has created generations of musicians who sound alike. We teach the same scales, the same chords and the process of combining the two in the same general manner. Students should have the luxury of choice about the way they want to personalize their playing, which a uniform approach stifles. They are faced with a variety of points of view about a single subject. When I was a student we had to learn them all. If we, as educators, have as our goal the development of individual voices, ideally then, there should be as many different voices as there are players. Every student should be exposed to multiple approaches to the theory and practice of playing jazz, making their own choices of what concepts fit their individual ways of playing. The process of learning how to play is rarely that of starting out with a strong, clear conception of how we want to play. It's a process of self-discovery and trial and error, trying out different musical ideas, theories, and concepts to discover our own individual voices. Quite often it's a matter of "finding out where we don't want to be," through a process of elimination. *Forward Motion* may not answer the question "how do I want play?" It will, at least, give you another point of view to consider. Take from it what works for you and throw out the rest.

How can naïve and inexperienced jazz students tell the difference between a good and a bad book?

They can't. Not without buying and reading them and trying out their suggestions. Even then it may be difficult to tell whether the book is worthwhile. The problem is that it's easy to make up almost any kind of theory, make it sound logical, put it into book form and sell it. Selling music information is a profitable venture, if not for the author, certainly for the publisher.

Publisher Charles Colin once confided in me that young jazz students buy every jazz book published, especially if it's related to a particular instrument and more so if the author has a reputation. Put out a drum book, every young drummer will buy it. These books are written and published for many reasons: profit, self-promotion, university tenure requirements of publish or perish, protection of individual research by copyright, historical documentation and as educational aids.

What makes a good jazz instruction book?

Two answers: First, if you got one usable idea out of it, it was a good book. If you get two or more usable ideas out of it it's a great book. Hopefully, the readers of *Forward Motion* will be able to find at least one good idea in it.

Second: A good jazz instruction book adheres to five to rigid standards that validates its concepts:

1. Its concepts can be historically validated by their previous use in the tradition of the music. The chain of how a concept grew and was

modified through the passage of time should be clear and unassailable. What worked in Bach's time in Germany must also work in Armstrong's time in New Orleans.

2. Its concepts are based upon sound scientific principles, i.e., how the mind, body and emotions function in the process of learning and making music.

3. Valid musical concepts must be applicable in any musical genre irrespective of time and place. They must encompass ideas that are universals.

4. It has to work. The concepts must be pragmatic.

5. Concepts must have the "Ring of Truth" for the student. Feelings about practicing and performing that are felt on an intuitive level, when then verbalized, create a sense of recognition. I can't count the number of times a student has said "Gee Hal, I felt something like that but didn't know what it meant." The challenge every educator faces is how to impart these concepts to the student without constricting the development of their individual styles.

Can anyone learn how to play jazz from a book?

No. The only function jazz education can serve, in any of its forms, is to stimulate your mind. To teach you how to teach yourself. Learning how to play jazz is essentially a self-taught process. Always has been and always will be. No one can teach you how to play. You can't learn how to play jazz by taking a four-year college course. It takes a lifetime of work to accomplish that goal. What jazz education offers is the opportunity to create and organize your own individual self-teaching methodology. The methodology you develop to learn how to play will eventually have a direct influence on your style of playing, your individual voice. If you want to develop your own individual voice you have to develop your own individual way of studying and practicing.

There are however, universals involved in practicing and playing that each student will encounter. These universals could be defined as the "whats" and "hows" of music.

The "whats" of music are factual and genre specific; the various aspects of harmony, melody, and rhythm as applicable to a particular genre or style of music. The "whats" are the smallest amount of musical information one needs to learn. The "hows" of musical ideas are universal in nature and take a lifetime to learn. Seymour Fink in his article "*Can You Teach Musicality*" (May/June 1997 issue of *Piano & Keyboard Magazine*), defines these two processes as " conscious factual knowledge (knowing what to do)" and " procedural knowledge (knowing how to do it)."

The "whats" are intellectual in content. The "hows" are experiential and usually learned through direct and continued playing experience. The only way to learn the "hows," or how to play what you play, is by performing it. Getting on the bandstand, night after night, with better musicians than you so you're constantly hearing it being played right, trying to get it right by trial and error.

In *Forward Motion* I've attempted to achieve the goal of keeping the intellectual aspects of learning how to play within the scope and context of the oral tradition and the aforementioned scientific principles. In that way students will be encouraged to focus more, on not only the mere information herein, but the processes involved with learning and applying that information.

Problems playing music can be reduced to difficulties that lay within the realm of mental states of mind such as: perception, conception and attitude. Consequently, this is a theory book only in how it relates to changing those states of mind. It is designed to alter a student's perception of music. What this book is not, is an exercise book. FM is tailored for the intermediate to advanced level musician, credit is given that the reader has the wherewithal to extrapolate the enclosed musical examples into exercises of their own.

INTRODUCTION

"The more upbeats you have in the music the more it swings"

Dizzy Gillespie

My original three articles on *Forward Motion* were published in Down Beat Magazine in 1980 & 1981. Their purpose was to show how melodies work as well as offering a way of practicing scales more in the manner they are used than in the way they were originally learned. Since that time my understanding of the subject has grown and the way I use FM in my teaching has been modified. Originally, I used FM to correct what I saw as a technical and theoretical problem. Now I see FM exercises as being used to correct what are basically perceptual problems. As most problems with playing music are perceptual in nature, to change the way you play you have to change the way you think.

When the articles were first published, I was sure I had come upon original research that no one else had duplicated. It wasn't until I read Albert Schweitzer's biography of Bach (*J.S. Bach, Vol. 1 & 2, Dover Books*) that I realized that the musical laws inherent in FM were universal. Anyone exploring this subject would come to the same conclusions that Bach and I did. The rules that govern music are universal, not affected by the passage of time, place or genre. There are concrete reasons why some music sounds better than others.

In volume 1, Pg. 312 of the Schweitzer biography is his analysis of Bach's concept of phrasing. "If we follow the principle indicated by Bach's manner of writing his phrases, we see that he usually conceives four consecutive notes as grouped in such a way that the first is detached from the others by an imperceptible break, and belongs rather to the previous group than to the one that follows." Thus not

but

He gives the following phrasing example from Bach's "Prelude in A Minor" (Peters II, No. 8):

On page 375 of the same volume (referring to Rudolf Westphal's metrical study of the fugues in Bach's *Well-tempered Clavichord*) "...he proves again and again that those who regard the bar-lines in Bach's music as the borders of the rhythmic factors are bound to play him un-rhythmically. In a Bach theme **everything surges forward to a principal accent**. (Emphasis mine). Till this comes all is restless, chaotic; when it arrives the tension relaxes, and at one stroke all that went before becomes clear, - we understood why the notes had these intervals and these values." And again, on page 396 of volume 2 "If we do not experience this sense of tension followed by relief, the theme has not been properly played; it has been phrased in the ordinary rhythm of the bars, instead of in its fundamental rhythm."

Beginning with our earliest childhood education a tacit conditioning occurs. We see "one" of the bar before we see any other beat or note. We count first beat of the bar as "one." Since "one" is the first number of the number series, years of perceiving music this way has conditioned us into thinking of "one" as the first beat of the bar. It would then seem logical that melodic phrases begin on the first beat of the bar, or "one."

However, Tension and Release Theory states that "one" of the bar is the strongest beat of the bar and as such, is the ultimate resolution beat in the bar. "Resolution" means that something has ended, consequently "one" of the bar **is not the first beat of the bar**; it is the **last beat of the bar**. It is the beat toward which melodic ideas are played and at which they end.

FM is based on the physical laws of sound and rhythm. These laws are immutable and as applicable in Bach's time as in ours. FM is also based upon the physiology of how the ear functions, another universal. The mind loves logic and rejects chaos. It has an innate tendency to want to make sense out of chaos. When faced with a problem or something that doesn't make sense, it automatically tries to make sense out of it by relating it to the familiar.

Such is the case, for example, when looking at a modern abstract painting by Klee. The mind tries to force the eye into making sense out of it by looking for ways to make the painting's content fall into recognizable representational objects: cars, trains, houses, animals, etc., as one does when looking at clouds. This same tendency is present in the ear as well. The ear tends to reject chaos and has a marked tendency to automatically make sense of the sounds it hears. To the ear, tension is intolerable and needs to be resolved. Have you noticed the problems you have going from one melodic fragment to another? How you have a hard time "hooking up" your ideas from one to the other? That's probably because you're starting your melodies on "one" and/or "three" of the bar. "One" is a resolution beat, a point of rest for the ear and stops the line. When starting a melody on a tension beat, the ear wants to resolve the tension by jumping ahead to its nearest resolution beat. If you start on the "and" of "two," your ear will want to hear towards the resolution on the up-coming beat, "three" of the bar.

FM is a practicing technique that takes advantage of this innate tendency to hear an idea in motion toward future rhythmic and harmonic resolution points. This ability can be developed to a highly sophisticated degree.

All art is the projection of an illusion created by the artist. This is no less so for the musician. When listening to a jazz solo, it is perceived in a static fashion. You are being subjected to an illusion. However, the player is hearing their melodic lines differently than the listener, as melodies and rhythms in motion toward future resolution points. Instead of hearing in a static manner, the soloist is hearing ahead of where they are in the music at the moment.

The ear can be trained to hear: two beats, four beats, two bars, eight bars ahead. The great jazz drummer, Billy Hart, once confided to me that he "hears" his whole chorus in approach to "one" of the next chorus. Since this is a natural innate ability, anyone can learn to hear and play in FM.

FORWARD MOTION IS DIVIDED INTO TEN CHAPTERS:

Melody and Embellishment creates a historical context for the following chapters by creating a framework for understanding how the process of jazz improvisation became increasingly more sophisticated from its beginnings in the early 1900's. It explains the historical connection between how it was done then and how it is still done today, clarifies those aspects of improvising that have changed and those that haven't and why.

Rhythmic *Forward Motion* introduces the basic concept of *Forward Motion*, starting with how my study of it began and how music is almost universally taught "backwards" from the way it really functions. It describes the functions of Tension and Release patterns rhythmically and melodically and how they can be played to create strong melodies that "spell" the changes out. This chapter also includes a discussion of playing in half time and its effect upon a player's conception of playing in tempo ending with a short treatise on Rhythmic Syncopation.

Scalar *Forward Motion* applies *Forward Motion* techniques to scale lines and how "Key Scales" can be transformed into "Chord Scales." Three categories of scales lines are discussed: scale lines that descend for chords of two beats duration, scale lines that ascend for chords of two beat's duration, and scale lines that ascend and descend for chords of four or more beats duration. The chapter illustrates the almost infinite ways that chord tones can be synchronized with the strong beats of the bar to clearly "spell" out chord changes. The use of Inner Guide Tone Melodies is also discussed.

Arpeggios and *Forward Motion* elaborates on how to add pickups and resolutions to arpeggios giving them a feeling of motion demonstrating the difference between themes that are in and out of *Forward Motion*. It then applies the technique of Melodic Inversion to insure you have explored all the possible ways arpeggios of different lengths can be combined.

Appoggiaturas and *Forward Motion* shows how chromatic embellishments can be synchronized to spell out chord changes. An abbreviated list of some of the infinite ways chromatic embellishments have been used in the jazz vocabulary is included.

Intervals and *Forward Motion* adds pickups and resolutions to large intervals (broken arpeggios) to give them a feeling of motion including examples of their use by modern composers and how they might be used in a solo context.

Harmonic *Forward Motion* details the advanced technique of spelling out chord changes in advance of where they are written and how to make them work within a solo line. It illustrates how current transcriptional analysis leads to misconceptions about how a soloist has spelled out the chord changes.

***Forward Motion* and Pentatonics and Cells** applies *Forward Motion* techniques to pentatonic scales, arpeggios and "Cell Playing" as well as how to delineate their **Inner Guide Tone Melodies**.

Superimposition is an advanced technique describing how musical freedom from the predictable elements of music: meter, harmony, melody and form can be achieved. Otherwise known as "being able to play anything anywhere," it illustrates how the masters used these elements only as guides to made up their own solo content over the predictable elements to create rhythmic and melodic freedom during a solo.

How To Practice *Forward Motion* debunks mechanical "repetition" as an outmoded practicing process. It offers a step-by-step process for retraining your hearing to hear in *Forward Motion*.

THE ORAL TRADITION:

Unlike western music, jazz's roots derive from the African oral tradition. In western cultures information is transmitted from generation to generation by the written word In African culture, information, such as stories, family history, music, social customs and laws, are handed down through succeeding generations by the spoken word and demonstration. Western music is taught in a classroom environment. Concepts are broken down to their smallest increments, analyzed to yield their meaning, then reconstituted to recreate the whole concept.

African music is taught in the Master/Student format. The student lives with the master, cleans his house, cooks, does his laundry. The student, through daily contact with the master, absorbs the master's thought processes. One-on-one individual lessons are the norm. The master plays a musical idea, for an example, a rhythmic pattern like: Dum, Dum, De, Dum, De De Dum, instructing the student to "make it sound like this." The music is taught by demonstration and copying. Copying not only what the master played but also how the master played it. This defines the crucial difference between the western and African teaching methodology. Western methodology interposes the intellectual process of theory and analysis between the teacher and student. The

African methodology involves the student directly in the sound and the feel of the music, bypassing the intellect by the process of copying. The western process is standardized, often stifling the development of one's original voice. The African process stimulates and encourages this development.

Africa's cultural history is handed down through succeeding generations by story telling. Each new generation tends to embellish their recitations. Each new version of the stories are imbued with their own individual idiosyncrasies. In this manner, the style in which the story is told may be personalized but **its true meaning is never altered**. Value is not only placed on remaining true to the basic traditional meaning of the story but on each story teller presenting these traditions in their own individual voice.

Similarly, a jazz musician's two primary goals are to not only absorb the traditions of the music but to develop their own individual musical voice as well. Copying, imitation, "make it sound like this," insures that both goals are achieved simultaneously. For this reason, the process of copying has remained the central process for learning how to play jazz.

Jazz musicians of earlier decades didn't have available to them the awesome amount of music information that is available to contemporary jazz students. Their instructional resources were limited to the radio, live performances, recordings and the apprenticeship system. In those days the only way the music could be learned was by trying to emulate the music of the masters by copying them. The result was that, as in African story telling, each new generation learned the tradition of the music but played the tradition, each in their own individual voices. One might postulate that it was the very lack of this information that created the strong identifying stylistic characteristics of the early generations of jazz musicians.

Music sounds good because the "rules" of the music were used correctly. Music sounds bad because they weren't. Consequently, if one copies good sounding musical ideas from the tradition of the music, one is learning the rules of how to play good music on an intuitive, not an intellectual level. Copying gets the student directly into the sound and vocabulary of the music. The history of the jazz vocabulary contains the rules of the music within it. Most of the great masters I had the good fortune to apprentice with throughout my career learned by copying and played by ear. Most, if asked to name what they played, couldn't. But they could show you how to play by hearing them night after night, playing it right, so you could hear it and through the process of trial and error, eventually emulate their playing. In this manner the history of the tradition was retained through newer generations. Each newer generation found their individual way to play it without altering its basic verities and as in African story telling, retained its true meaning.

As this music is learned by listening and copying, then understanding what you are hearing and copying it is a crucial element of the learning process. *Forward Motion* insures that you are hearing the music correctly by copying and practicing it correctly.

"Attitude Is Everything" (Jazz Proverb)

Webster's Dictionary defines the word "proverb" as "a maxim of wisdom... An allegorical saying of the wise that requires interpretation." The roots of jazz music are firmly planted in the oral tradition of African music. The oral tradition is the process masters of the music used to efficiently pass musical wisdom down to succeeding generations of musicians. This wisdom is usually experiential and difficult to record in written form. Jazz proverbs are ubiquitous throughout the history of jazz and are very powerful. They function on a conceptual level. The information they contain is experiential in nature, embodying enormous amounts information that, after much reflection by the student and guidance from a master, illuminate the subject. After lengthy consideration, they have the effect of changing a musician's mental, emotional and physical

25

actions; their mental states, attitudes, conceptions and perceptions, the way musicians think and feel about themselves, the music and their relationships to their instrument, practice, performance and other players. They effect musical behavior achieving global, as opposed to incremental, changes upon their playing.

Over the years, both through research and personal experience apprenticing with the masters, I have concentrated my efforts on collecting, analyzing and explicating these jazz proverbs to unlock the information they contain. All my writings are derived from my investigations into this rapidly vanishing and most valuable resource. It's the nature of these proverbs that you may not gain a complete understanding of it's meaning for decades. They are perceived at first as being one-dimensional. They sound logical but the information in them is hidden. Their other dimensions are illuminated only after one has had enough experience and acquired enough knowledge to relate to the proverb personally. Throughout this book, I have used jazz proverbs, quoted both from jazz masters and of my own creation, followed by their explication. The greatest challenge that I, as author, and you as reader face, is my capability to not only explain these proverbs but to impact their meaning to the reader on a gut level, to change the way you think.

MELODY AND EMBELLISHMENT

"Learn how to play a melody before you do all them fancy embellishments." **Joe "King" Oliver to Louis Armstrong**

Joe Oliver's advice distinguishes between two different types of improvisation; melodic and embellishment. His intuitively founded concept is based upon a fundamental scientific principle about how the ear works, particularly when a musician "plays by ear." (King Oliver was, it should be noted, an "ear player.") This being: complexity is based upon a foundation of simplicity. If one can't hear and execute simple musical ideas then one hasn't yet established in the ear the foundation required upon which to execute more complex ideas. In his study of the relationship between mental processes and the playing of music (*The Art of Piano Playing: A Scientific Approach,* Summy-Birchard), George Kochevitsky presented convincing evidence that virtually all music is played "by ear."

Douglas Hofstadter, in his Pulitzer Prize winning book: "*Godel, Escher, Bach,"* (Vintage Books) suggests that the ear hears in a linear (horizontal) fashion, from line to line, idea to idea, as opposed to a "stacked" (linear) fashion. As an example, he sites the experience of listening to a Bach

CHAPTER 1

four-part fugue. The listener can't perceive all the parts at once, on the same level. The ear can hear a fugue in either one of two ways: As soon as the ear selects a particular line of the fugue, the others recede into the background. When trying to hear the sum of the four parts at the same time, the ear can only perceive the total as an aural "color."

This concept that the mind works in a linear fashion is also supported by Robert *Jourdain's* book "*Music, The Brain, And Ecstasy,*" (William Morrow). Jourdain states that the mind works in stream of "perceptual chunks," going from "chunk to chunk" in nanoseconds so small that the conscious mind is unaware of their passing.

Similarly, the ear tends to select one of the four chord tones of each chord as the chord changes progress through a tune. Or, the chords are heard as a "color," such as the "altered" color, or the "Major 7th, #11" color. (Color hearing is an advanced way of hearing that is usually developed after many years of ear training and experience.) A player eventually begins to hear a chord tone not as a "named note," for example, as a flat 7th as such, but as the "color" of a flat 7th.

The current standardized pedagogy of teaching jazz improvisation as a process of merely synchronizing scales with their appropriate chord symbols, is only a "short-cut" for learning how to improvise. This approach is based upon principles neither scientifically nor musically sound. Jazz chord changes have four basic chord tones: the root, 3rd, 5th and 7th. We are taught to think of these tones as moving through a tune in a vertical manner, as if all the chord tones can be heard separately and together at the same time. As the scientific research suggests, this is impossible. The ear can only hear one way at a time, in a linear fashion. To clarify this concept, I'll define melody and embellishment in specific ways.

In the earlier decades of the 1900's improvised solos were created using the melodies of the songs of the period; "let the melody be your guide" being the operative principle. Most of these songs were written in a "simple" manner so they were singable to the listener ("All The Things You Are," "Autumn Leaves," for example). The rhythmic content of these melodies were, for the most part, inactive-composed of mostly Whole-notes, Half-notes. and sometimes quarter-notes and constructed using basic chord-tones (roots, 3rds, 5ths, and 7ths).

"Melodic" ideas can then be defined as being rhythmically inactive and constructed of chord tones. It follows then that "Embellishments" can be defined as being rhythmically active (8th notes, triplets, and 16th notes, etc.) and constructed of non-chord-tones (either in the key or "tension" notes outside the key).

Rhythmically Inactive	Whole Notes, Half Notes, sometimes Quarter-notes. Any of the above tied together or combined. Rests in any combination of the above Unanticipated rhythms ("On beats").
Rhythmically Active	Sometimes Quarter-notes, Eighth Notes, Triplets and 16th notes. Any of the above tied together or combined. Rests in any combination of the above Anticipated rhythms ("Off Beats").
Melodically Inactive	Basic chord tones: Roots, Thirds, Fifths and Sevenths.
Melodically Active	Non-Chord tones, Chord Extensions-Substitutions and/or Roots, Thirds, and Fifths of Super-Imposed triads.

To create interest, these variables can be combined in any manner.

You've probably been hearing this aspect of soloing while listening to the Masters improvise without making distinctions between melodic lines in terms of their active and inactive melodic and rhythmic content. Try listening to solo's making these distinctions between melody and embellishment. Notice that each player has his or her own particular mix of active and inactive content. Their styles can even be partially defined by each player's individual mix of melodic and embellished lines.

Oliver makes a value judgement that melodic lines are more important than embellished lines. He is addressing the universal predisposition of younger players to give precedence in their minds to faster, active and "flashier" melodic content over slower and more melodic inactive melodies. I know it was true for me. A case in point:

I remember my first big band combo my first semester at Berklee. Everybody was in the band room warming up before the rehearsal. There was this one guy, a tenor player, who was playing into a corner of the room with his back to the others. He was running up and down his horn playing all these fast lines and, in my naiveté, I was impressed. I remember thinking "Wow, I sure would like to be able to play all that someday." There's a natural, inbred, tendency for young players to be impressed with the flashier aspects of improvising. Oliver's statement directly addresses this issue by trying to reduce the value we give to these active lines and increase the value given to inactive lines.

This re-evaluation is accomplished by considering faster lines as "bridges" or "connectors" between slower lines. Melodic lines can start as active melodies and end with inactive melodies, and visa versa. Certain aspects of Tension and Release come into play at this point.

Playing only melodic content for a certain amount of time will create tension that needs to be released by its opposite, active content. Conversely, active content, played for a certain amount of time, creates tension that needs to be released by its opposite, melodic content. Rests, continued for too long, create tension that needs to be resolved by its opposite and the same goes for lines with no rests. The balance between these elements is a matter of personal taste and style.

Oliver is suggesting that you can't successfully improvise active lines without first developing the ability to improvise interesting and melodic inactive lines. You'll notice in the following chapters on *Forward Motion* that all active melodies are built around inactive Guide Tone melodies. The ear has a natural tendency to hear from simple to complex. To establish a clear foundation upon which to hear and understand more rhythmically and melodically complex musical ideas, the ear of the improviser (as well as that of the listener) desires to hear a simple melody first. To paraphrase Oliver, improvising by ear is easier when you have established something simple and clear around which to improvise. (Again, "let the melody be your guide.")

An appraisal of the history of jazz improvisation over the decades demonstrates that the melodic content of solos has decreased and the embellishments increased to the point that melodic content would seem to have disappeared, making the "let the melody be your guide" advice apparently irrelevant to today's improvisers. This is not the case. The melodic content is still there. It has, over time, been assumed and is less obvious than in the earlier decades of the music. The process of improvising around simple, hearable, inactive melodies is still occurring, but on a more sophisticated level. These assumed melodies are made of the basic chord-tones (or superimposed chord-tones, the roots, 3rds 5ths of superimposed triads) of the changes as they move through a tune. As opposed to being limited to embellishing a song's melodies, contemporary improvisers now have the freedom to choose their own chord-tone melodies (5th to 3rd, to root, to 7th to 5th etc.) from the infinite possibilities of combinations inherent in the changes.

What Oliver is suggesting is, if **you can't improvise your own inactive "song-like" chord-tone melodies, you haven't established a firm foundation in your ears upon which to improvise more active musical ideas (embellishments).** If "the melody is your guide," the only way one can improvise through tunes constructed of embellishments themselves (such as Charlie Parker's "Confirmation" or "Ornithology," tunes which have melodies too active to embellish, is to learn to hear and use the internal guide-tone melodies upon which faster lines are based. To establish this firm foundation in your hearing takes an extraordinary amount of patience. The tendency to gravitate toward

CHAPTER 1

practicing only faster lines must be resisted. This tendency exists because you haven't yet developed a full appreciation for melodic improvising. Once you have this appreciation you'll enjoy playing melodic content to a much greater degree. See if you can improvise a melodic line (it must have an aspect of sing-ability) using only Half-notes made exclusively out of basic chord tones. For example:

Example 1:

Try this exercise on every tune you know. This will confirm whether you really know the changes to the tunes. (Pianists call this kind of chord tone motion voice leading, i.e., the various ways chord tones of a chord can move smoothly to the chord tones of the next chord).

The nature of strong melodic content, whether composed or improvised, by Bach or Bird, has historically been created by the embellishment of chord-tones and, whether we are aware of it or not, still is. For example, the following excerpt (from page 29 of Bert Ligon's excellent book: *Connecting Chords with Linear Harmony*, published by Hal Leonard, available on amazon.com) of Bach's Prelude, "English Suite in G Minor," uses chord-tone melodies of Example #1's changes,

Scale vs. Chord-Tone Improvising

It was mentioned earlier that the aural memory tends to retain logical ideas and tends to reject illogical ones. The ear perceives patterns as

CHAPTER 1

being logical. One of our practicing goals is the development of patterned hearing.

It's often difficult to hear a melodic line from 8th note to 8th note. The notes go by too fast. Conversely, it's just as difficult to hear a complete melodic idea before it is played. Improvisers make a compromise between the two and train themselves to hear in patterns. As the ear perceives them as logical, they are easily retained in the aural memory. By playing a series of patterned melodies, the improviser acquires the ability to string them together to create the illusion of a long melodic line. As you become a more advanced improviser, you'll use patterned hearing in a different way, a subject for another book in itself. The following examples demonstrate how patterns and chord-tone melodies are used to navigate through chord changes to create strong melodic content as well as how to improvise with discipline and freedom, two concepts which at first appear to be mutually exclusive.

Example 2 below is a sample of a long melodic line on a standard set of "Rhythm" changes. They are beamed to create the visual illusion of a long melodic line.

Example 2:

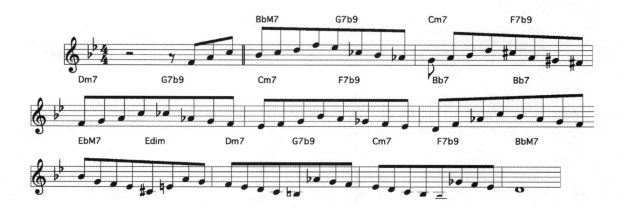

The next example is notated using *Forward Motion* Notation. It shows how a long line is conceived by the player as a series of smaller, 4-note patterns strung together, and smoothed out (by not accenting the notes on "1" and "3" of the bars) to create the illusion of a long line. Each group starts on a Tension Beat and moves toward the Target Notes on the Release Beats of the bars.

Example 3:

In example 4 the Target Notes are isolated from the line to show the inner Target Note Melody around which the melodic line is constructed.

Example 4:

Analysis of Inner Target Note Melody

(Bar #1) The Root of the BbMaj., to the 5th of a super-imposed Ab- triad on the G Alt. to

(Bar #2) the 5th of the C-7, to the 5th of a super-imposed F# triad on the F7 Alt. to

(Bar #3) the 3rd of the D-7 to the 3rd of the G7b9 to

(Bar #4) the 3rd of the C-7 to the 3rd of the F7b9 to

(Bar #5) the 3rd of the Bb7 to the root of the Bb7 to

(Bar #6) the 5th of the EbMaj. to the 3rd of a super-imposed A triad to

(Bar #7) the 3rd of the D-7 to the 3rd of the G7b9 to

(Bar #8) the 3rd of the C-7 to the root of a super-imposed Diminished 7th chord to

(Bar #9) the 3rd of the BbMaj.

This is the guide tone melody that helps you hear through the changes. Play it by itself before trying to play the complete line. If you can't retain the complete 8 bars, try it in shorter segments. Always starting from the first bar, add more segments until you can hear and play the complete melodic line for 8 bars.

All problems with playing are hearing problems. When having trouble playing any melodic line always play the last note(s), the Target Note(s) first, this gives the ear a place to hear toward (See the chapter: Practicing *Forward Motion*).

CHAPTER 1

The next 8-bar example demonstrates the fallacy of scale-wise improvisation. Using the same Target Notes as in Example 4, you'll find the approaches made of notes completely out of the chord scale. Yet, when the approaches end on the Target Notes, even though sometimes out of the key, they still sound good. An explanation of why this works will follow. The accompanying chords should fall on "1" and "3" of the bar. This is a somewhat extreme version of the process but it should serve to illuminate the melodic freedom that can be possible when using chord tone melodies to improvise.

Example 5:

Combining the strong tones of a chord, synchronizing them with the strong beats of the bar, "justifies" the tension notes that precede them. Try experimenting doing this with wide intervals, of any notes, inside or outside the key. It still works. Combining the discipline of knowing your chord tone melodies with the freedom of playing any approach to them shows that discipline and freedom are not inconsistent. Acquiring a firm grasp of how a chord tone of a chord can go to a chord tone of the next is the basis of the theory of counterpoint.

Your goal is to establish, at an early stage of your development, the ability to hear and create song-like chord-tone melodies and then learn how to embellish them.

Oliver makes the value judgement that certain melodies and notes are more important than others; that melodic content is of primary importance and embellishments are of secondary importance. He de-emphasizes the historical tendency of young players to play fast lines - without having done the proper preparation to execute them well. He is saying that, for your music to be more accessible, you must also consider the listener's ears and what those ears require.

It is common advice that a solo should "tell a story." If you start your solo with too much activity you'll have no place to go with it. By beginning with slower melodic ideas you bring the ear of the listener into your solo. Start your solos with lines of melodic content and progress to faster lines, using them to connect melodic ideas. Cannonball once advised me: "Start and end your solos with clear ideas that the listener can hear.

CHAPTER 1

Involving the listener in your playing is the soloist's responsibility."

As you progress through the succeeding chapters of *Forward Motion* you'll notice how completely Melody and Embellishment interlocks with every aspect of the FM concept.

This linear/harmonic approach to chord-like thinking is rarely taught. Once you have learned the chords to a tune and can visualize them, you then learn that any chord tone of one chord can move to any chord tone of the following chord These exercises begin with the most common (and basic) example of linear chord-tone motion, going to the strongest tones in a chord, the 3rds.

Learn and hear the internal Guide Tone Melody, which in this example,is a progression of 3rds moving through the chord changes. Practice this melody until you can hear it. Once you've reached a point where you are relatively familiar with the sound of this motion begin to add Embellishments to the chord tone melody by approaching each tone by an 8th note from either a scale tone above or a half-step below. This exercise must be played in tempo without stopping.

Example 6: Adding an Embellishment from a scale step above

Example 7: Adding an Embellishment from a half-step below

When adding a single approach from below a chromatic approach seems smoother than a scale step approach.

Example 8: Mixing and alternating the Embellishments from above and below in two versions

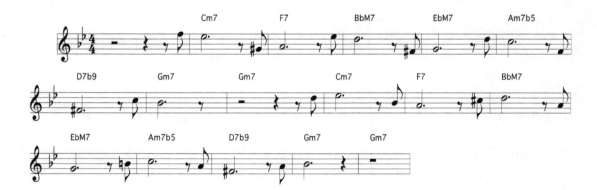

Example 9: Two-note Embellishments from above

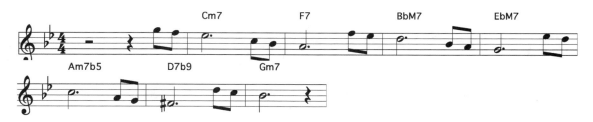

Example 10: Two-note Embellishments from below

Create an exercise extending the two-note approach exercise by alternating two-note Embellishments from above and below as was done in Example 8.

Example 11: Three-note Embellishments from above

Create an exercise extending the three-note approach exercise by alternating three-note Embellishments from above and below as in Example 8.

At this point we're beginning to incorporate the ascending and descending four-note groups exercises as discussed in the chapters on *Forward Motion*.

By this time you should have noticed that we didn't select enough basic chord-tones from each chord to create a consecutive 8th note line.

This is achieved by adding more two rules:

Rule #1: Chords having a duration of two beats each will contain only one Inner Guide Tone melody per chord.

Example 12:

Rule #2: Chords having a duration of four beats each will contain two Inner Guide Tone melodies per chord. Some of the chord tones may repeat.

Example 13:

Rule #3: Chords having a duration of two bars each will have four Inner Guide Tone melodies per chord. Chord tones will repeat.

CHAPTER 1

Example 14:

RHYTHMIC *FORWARD MOTION*

While a student at Berklee School of Music in the mid '50's, for some instinctual reason I became preoccupied trying to understand the nature of "one" of the bar. It seemed important to me although at the time I didn't know why.

During this period I bought the album "Everybody Digs Bill Evans." The title came from the fact that the album cover was filled with testimonials from great jazz musicians about Bill's playing. Cannonball's testimonial hit a nerve. He said: "Bill's Evans has rare originality and taste and the even rarer ability to make his conception of a number seem the definitive way to play it." It was the word "definitive" that stuck out to me. If what Cannon said was true, this meant that there were reasons why some tunes sounded better than others, and by extension, reasons why some lines sound better than others. Wanting to play the most definitive melodies myself, I began my research by trying to analyze why some melodic lines sound better than others. I started with a series of questions and their answers.

What defines a definitive line?

Answer: A line that is strong.

What defines a strong line?

CHAPTER 2

Answer: A line that spells out the chord changes (either basic or superimposed) so clearly you can hear the harmony without a chord being played behind it.

How do melodic lines spell out chord changes?

Using the system of Tension and Release analysis the obvious became clear:

Answer: By synchronizing the strong beats of the bar with the strong tones of a chord and the weak beats of the bar with weak tones.

The Release beats of a bar ("one" & "three" and the "on" beats of every quarter-note) are the strong beats of the bar. The Tension beats of the bar ("two" & "four" and the "ands" of each quarter-note) are the weak beats of the bar. The Release tones of a chord scale are the root, third, fifth & seventh. They are the strong tones of the chord scale. The non-chord tones are the weak tones. (Note: When analyzing chord extensions: 9, b9, #9, 11, #11, b13, etc. the notes that fall on the release beats will be found to be either the root, third & fifth of a superimposed triad. For example: The C# on a C7 can be called a b9. As a superimposed chord it could be called the third of an A triad. More on this subject in the chapter on "Superimposition."

When synchronized, the "on" beats of the bar and the chord tones have a natural emphasis within them that are enhanced. This emphasis "spells out" the chord tones of the changes. When chord tones (basic or superimposed) are synchronized with the "on" beats of the bar, the chord changes are being "spelled out" by the melodic line. The melodies become so strong that even without a chord being played behind them, you can hear the movement of the chords as they progress through a tune.

For example: Every musician knows that the F major scale is common to the II-V-I of the key of F. Many beginning improvisers use this understanding to improvise scale-wise. They realize that as long as the piano or guitar player is playing the chord changes for G-7- C7- Fmaj., they can just run the scale and sound more or less like they are improvising in the key. However as soon as the accompanying chords are removed from the background, the melodies sound weak because they are unsynchronized.

To understand the difference between rhythms that are in and out of *Forward Motion*, try this experiment: (T=Tension, R=Release).

Counting two bars of 4/4, sing the example below, calling "1" and "3" of the bars "Do" and "2" and "4" of the bars "Wa." Repeat these two bars, at a medium tempo, without stopping.

CHAPTER 2

Example 1:

Stop the tempo and, counting off seven beats outside the bar, call the beats on "4" and "2" "Do" and "1" and "3" of the bars "Wa."

Example 2:

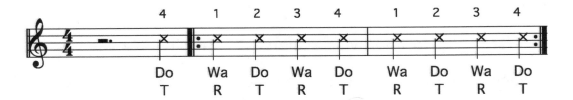

Stop the tempo and switch back to example #1 again. You'll notice example #2 swings more than #1. Switch back and forth between examples a few times so that the different feeling of each becomes clear to you.

Now try this using 8th notes.

Example 3:

Counting off four beats outside the bar at the same tempo as the other examples, calling the on beats "Do" and the off beats "Wa," repeating the two bars.

Stop the tempo, count off and start again calling the off beats "Do" and the on beats "Wa." Repeat without stopping.

Example 4:

Notice how example #4 swings more than example #3. It has a little hop in it that we are all familiar with. Most beginning improvisers attempt to get this hop in an artificial manner, through articulation, by either playing their eight notes: loud-soft-loud-soft, or long-short-long short, rather than by playing the notes in the right place at the right time.

By this time the difference between playing rhythms in and out of FM should begin to be apparent to your ear.

CHAPTER 2

Playing In Half-Time

"The faster you play, the slower you count." - Dizzy Gillespie

Forward Motion has global effects upon the mind, body and emotions of the jazz improviser. One of FM's effects is that playing in *Forward Motion* requires you to think faster than usual. I use the word "think" with caution, to describe a particular kind of "thinking."

Mitch Haupers, in his article "The Musician Mind," (Berklee Today, Summer 1994) quoting from Howard Gardner's "Creating Minds "(Basic Books 1993), makes a clear distinction between two kinds of thinking; intelligence and creativity. "...intelligence and creativity are not the same. Intelligence is measured in terms of *convergent thinking* - the ability to give the 'correct' answer on an IQ test - while creativity stimulates *divergent thinking* - the tendency to respond to problems by searching for a wide range of possible interpretations." It is divergent thinking to which I'm referring.

Many of the childhood musical concepts we were taught were *apropos* for the time. Learning how to count in quarter-note time and where the notes were on the instrument were our first musical challenges. Learning where "one" of the bar was, and your basic scales usually accomplished these goals. In the process, we acquired a tacit conditioning of how music worked that is not *apropos* for adult musicians. Unawares, we accepted this conditioning as a truth; that "one" of the bar was the first beat of the bar and the root of a scale was its first note. **We were all taught backward**

Quarter-note time is what can be termed a "swing" beat. It has a dynamic, propulsive quality that makes it difficult to play by choice and with control. The operative attitude is that one must be exciting, not excited. Quarter-note time induces tension and creates over-excitement and compulsive 8th note playing, literally reducing instrumental facility by 50%. 8th notes played with an underlying quarter-note feeling have a forced, over-articulated quality. These difficulties occur for one reason only: quarter-note tempos occur at a rate of speed too fast to conceive and execute 8th note ideas. Reconditioning your attitude and conception of playing quarter-note time can eliminate this effect.

Use of quarter-note time is a hold over from childhood musical experience. All young music students must develop an internal "clock" and learn how to count tempo in steady quarter-notes. This concept is then mistakenly carried over into adult musical behavior. Although most childhood behavior becomes modified when reaching adulthood, somehow we think this is not true of many of our early musical concepts. Most of us feel our internal tempo "clock" in one of four ways: as steady quarter-

CHAPTER 2

notes, on 2 & 4 of the bar, on 1 & 3 of the bar or in a steady stream of syncopated rhythms. Defined as "Swing Beats", quarter-note time and 2 & 4 of the bar are emotionally charged beats. You snap your fingers on 2 & 4 because those beats swing. They are often used by player's as a "crutch" for keeping place and imparting a false feeling of swing to their ideas. Those who count using these beats have yet to reach rhythmic maturity. Learning to play in half time is adult rhythmic behavior.

The half-time approach to playing time can be applied to most tempos, except ballads. By altering your subjective perception of playing quarter-note time to playing in half time, you'll feel the tempo as being half as fast. You'll therefore be twice as relaxed, have twice as much time to conceive ideas and double your technical facility. In effect, you will be conceiving every tune as a ballad. It's impossible to become over-excited playing a ballad tempo.

Playing in half time synchronizes neatly with FM, allowing the player more time to think and the option of choice. Half time also synchronizes the target beats and target tones with the "on" beats of "one" & "three" of the bar.

You can experience the feeling of playing in half-time by trying the following experiment; tap your foot on beats 1 & 3 of a 4/4 tempo, counting every two beats as one beat of a tempo at half the speed of the 4/4 tempo and counting over two-bar phrases. You are then tapping out quarter-notes of a ballad (half time) tempo.

Play the following example of an 8 note, C Major "Bebop" scale, in the following manner: Begin by tapping your foot on every quarter-note at a medium-up, 4/4 tempo. Repeat the scale ascending and descending without stopping at the top or bottom of the scale.

Example 5:

After four or more bars, without stopping, change your foot tapping from each quarter-note to 1 & 3 of the bar, and continue play the scale. You'll be tapping your foot on every two beats of the two bar phrase.

Example 6:

Switch back and forth a few times. Notice the over-articulated quality of the scale while tapping Quarter-notes and how, when tapping on 1 & 3, it changes to a legato phrasing that is easier to execute. What has occurred is, by tapping on 1 & 3 you are now playing 8th notes that were originally in 4/4 as 16th notes in 2/2 and are, in effect, playing a ballad tempo.

Example 7:

Notice that the tempo marking of 90 in Example 7 is half as fast as the tempo marking 180 in Example 6. The result is that in Example 7 the melody sounds to the listener as 8th notes, but the player is conceiving them at a different rate of speed as 16th notes.

You may have experienced the feeling of playing in half time without realizing it. Have you noticed how easy it is to improvise 8th note ideas while playing a samba or bossa nova? Brazilian music is written and played in 2/2 and is based on the clave beat which is a two bar phrase. Have you noticed how easy it is to improvise double-time, 16th note ideas on a ballad? That's the half-time feeling at work.

Playing in half time has a particular feeling and quality of sound that many of the masters have achieved. This effect can be most clearly recognized when listening to their recordings of up-tempo tunes. The half time technique is most clearly demonstrated by a stride pianist's left hand. It is the only way to successfully execute the stride.

As when learning anything new, it will take time and practice to get used to this new and unfamiliar perception of time. You'll have to retrain years of conditioning of playing in quarter-note time. It will be especially difficult to resist slipping back into quarter-note time while playing with a drums and bass who must play with a quarter-note feeling. From time to time, you may switch back to quarter-note time playing for the sake of rhythmic variety and add extra propulsiveness to a line.

There are two potential hazards of playing in half time. First, don't switch the time values of the chord changes from 4/4 to half time, making the tune a virtual ballad. Secondly, avoid the tendency to play too far behind the beat.

Review and relearn your repertoire and play all your songs with a ballad concept; i.e., a 12 bar blues becomes a six bar ballad, a 32 bar tune becomes a 16 bar ballad, etc. You can also alter your perception of time by selecting a ballad you know well enough you that don't have to think about it while playing. After few bars begin to improvise double-time 16th note melodies. At the end of 16 bars, switch to a blues in another key at twice the tempo. Try to retain the legato, over-the-bar line feeling of the 16th notes in the faster quarter-note tempo. If you lose the feeling, return to the ballad and start again until you can make

CHAPTER 2

the switch without reverting back to quarter-note time.

From this point on your goal will be to eliminate feeling tempo in quarter-note time and 8th note playing from your conception of music. Listen to music while counting in half time. **All practicing of 8th notes lines should be mentally translated into 16th note lines in half time.**

Most of us have been conditioned into believing that jazz improvising should be hard work and feel that if it becomes easy we are somehow "cheating". Improvising should be fun. It can't be fun if it's not easy to do. Being used to working hard, it will be difficult getting used to playing being easy. When first learning how to play in half time, students often complain that they "don't feel like they're doing anything." That's the way it's supposed to feel.

Rhythmic Syncopation

"I fill my head with rhythm" Dizzy Gillespie

The most pervasive difficulty western jazz student's face is the lack of a true understanding of rhythmic syncopation. According to Dizzy Gillespie, in Mike Longo's interview with the master, this difficulty stems from the difference between the African and western concepts of rhythm: "...the African concept of rhythm is polyrhythmic and we are mono-rhythmic." Mr. Longo clarifies Dizzy's statement: "Poly-rhythm is a combination of several independent rhythmic melodies that agree vertically as well as horizontally. That is to say that even though these are horizontally independent melodies, they also mesh with each other from a vertical point of view, in what would seem like a form of rhythmic harmony."

In western society we are taught to learn time as being executed as a series of quarter-notes. However quarter-note time is unsophisticated and mechanical, what Dizzy calls "clock time." Rhythmic syncopation is sophisticated and complex, what Dizzy defines as "human time."

It was the African invention of syncopation that transformed western music into jazz. It was a rhythmic innovation. Yet, rhythmic syncopation, the musical element that makes jazz, jazz, is the least

CHAPTER 2

understood aspect of jazz. Syncopation is the life-blood of the music. It has magical qualities. Of all the inventions of the human mind none can be found comparable. Syncopation is a unique construct that allows individuals to be part of a group experience while at the same time retaining each participant's individuality. In most group endeavors it is usually either one or the other, being either part of a group with a consequent loss or individuality or the opposite, where one retains their individuality to the detriment of the total group experience. Only in jazz music, through the concept of rhythmic syncopation, do both successfully coexist.

I learned syncopation at the feet of the masters, by playing with them, hearing how it should go night after night, by trying my best to emulate it. Unfortunately, the masters I learned it from are dead and, because of the demise of the apprenticeship system, their disciples are not in a position to pass it on to others through the oral tradition. But there is hope.

I had the good fortune to spend a week with Dizzy when he was a guest artist with the Phil Woods Quintet in the 80's. I was never the same after that week. All Dizzy talked about for that week was rhythm, rhythm, and more rhythm. When the inventor of the music puts so much emphasis on one particular aspect of jazz, I got the point, that jazz is, at root, a rhythmic invention. If you don't understand the rhythm you don't understand the music.

"First, learn how to hear everything and play everything you hear, then hear everything and play as little of it as possible." (HG)

The development of "patterned hearing" was mentioned as one of an improviser's goals. The exercises in this book will mostly be continuous 8th note lines. Once you've learned how to hear and play a steady 8th note line you'll need a process to change the way you hear those lines. That process is syncopation. The following technique can only be implemented when you have acquired the ability to hear and execute a continuous 8th note line. Try the following suggestions before you have arrived at this level of expertise and it will not work as well.

The first stage of the process a jazz musician goes through is to develop a strong brain-to-hand signal that intuitively responds to what you hear. We spend the first half of our career learning how to hear all the different components of jazz improvising until we can play them as they occur in our ears. One of our goals is to be able to internalize the ability to hear a steady 8th note line and then the ability to play it

CHAPTER 2

without thinking. At this stage of development one usually becomes a "notey" player, lacking phrasing and space in one's solos. It takes a lot of time and work to acquire this ability. Being human, seeking rewards for our labors is understandable, especially after working hard to achieve this level of hearing. We don't want to give it up, continuing to play everything we hear. However, to achieve the more sophisticated rewards of playing on a more advanced level the improviser must deny themselves this low-level reward. As long as you settle for less you can't get more.

The next stage of development, the application of natural phrasing, syncopation and the use of space, requires a lifetime to achieve. Space is an illusion created by the performer. There is no such thing as space, only the illusion of it created by the performer not playing everything that is going on inside their head.

It is commonly thought that achieving this stage of playing is reached by a process of "editing" your melodic lines by leaving notes out. This is impossible as the lines are moving too fast to say "I think I'll leave these notes out of my line." By the time you've thought of it the line has long passed. The only way to achieve a more sophisticated level of improvising is to change the way you hear. This is achieved by substituting rhythmically syncopated hearing by letting the rhythms select which notes you want to play. To understand this process, try the following experiment.

Many students have learned the melodies of bebop heads melody first without having focused on their rhythmic aspect. When asked to sing the rhythms to the Charlie Parker tune "Confirmation", as if playing the rhythm of the tune on hollow log, they have difficulty doing so without singing the melody line along with the rhythms illustrating the fact that they really don't know the rhythmic basis of the tune.

Select a complex rhythmic bebop melody that you know really well, such as Confirmation. Sing the tune in a monotone (you may find this difficult if you haven't learned the tune from its rhythmic as well as melodic aspect), as if you were playing it on a drum. Do not sing any tones. Next, take the rhythm of Confirmation and apply it to soloing on another tune you know really well such as "Autumn Leaves" or "All The Things You Are." Don't think melodically. Let the rhythms of Confirmation select the notes you're going to play. After trying this a few times you'll be able to perceive this process in action.

The key to this advanced process is in the following statement by Dizzy: "You construct from a point of the rhythm. Melody conforms with what you have in your mind. How you want the rhythm to go. Then you put your notes to that. I think of rhythm first." (from a Dizzy interview

CHAPTER 2

with Mike Longo). The rhythms he's referring to are not the western mono-rhythms (i.e. quarter-note beats) but the African poly-rhythms.

In other words the key to playing syncopated phrases is to **think rhythmically instead of melodically. If you think of the rhythm first, the rhythm will automatically select the proper notes out of the continuous 8th note line that is running through your ears.** This requires trust in the fact that, without thinking about it, the continuous 8th note line is still operating in your ears.

Referring to the Dizzy quote at the beginning of the section, he fills his head with rhythm as in the clave beat as shown in example 7 or a syncopated flow of rhythms.

The next is an example of a 6/8 clave beat.

Example 8:

While the quarter-note beat in the bottom stave is going on you're thinking the 6/8 rhythm in your head. The syncopations in the top stave will "select" the proper notes from the continuous 8th note line that is going on in your head at the same time.

The next example bears some explanation.

It is generally considered that the articulation of 8th notes is played with a 12/8 inflection. However, if we're playing in half time, then every two bars of 12/8 translates into four bars of 6/8. The rhythmic inflections of 12/8 and 6/8 do not have the same feeling. You can try this out by imagining a 12/8 rhythm in your head while playing an 8th note line over it. Then try the same experiment with a 6/8 rhythm. You'll notice that the placement of your line within the flow of time differs with each experiment. The 6/8 "lays" better.

Play example 9 and try to find the quarter-note pulse.

Example 9: (Courtesy of Mike Longo)

Example 10: shows where the quarter-note pulse is. (Courtesy of Mike Longo)

CHAPTER 2

The quarter-note pulse is written in the second stave. Although written as 8th's with a quarter rest they are actually dotted quarters. Try playing an improvised line while keeping the rhythms in example 10 in your mind. Do not try to think melodically. See if the rhythm selects the notes for you. Dizzy's lesson is, when soloing, **always think rhythm first.**

SCALAR *FORWARD MOTION*

Strong and Weak Melodies

Scales are the raw material from which melodic ideas are drawn. **Improvising is the reordering of the notes of a scale into their strongest melodic possibilities**.

In the chapter on Rhythmic *Forward Motion*, tension and release patterns were used to define the strong and weak beats of the bar. When analyzing chord scales in terms of tension (weak) and release (strong) tones, the strong tones are the root, 3rd, 5th and 7th, the weak tones being the non-chord tones: 9, 11, 13 and any added half-steps.

A chord is spelled out by synchronizing the strong beats of the bar (the "on" beats) with the strong tones (chord tones) of a chord scale and the weak beats (the "off" beats) with the weak tones (non-chord tones).

"On" Beats = Release; "Off" Beats = Tension
Chord Tones = Release; Non-Chord-Tones = Tension

The strong beats are easier to hear than the weak ones. The strong tones are easier to hear than the weak ones. When synchronized they reinforce each other, further strengthening the soloists ability to "hear toward" basic chord tones (predictable) as well as "1" and "3" (predictable) of the bar from farther and farther in advance.

If a melodic line sounds weak, the reason will always be that the rhythmic and melodic tension-and-release patterns are "out of sync."

Scale lines with *Forward Motion* fall into three distinct categories, each with a slightly different set of rules. (The term "rules" is used in a relative sense: all rules are optional, depending on what's happening at the moment. They are operational while they are applicable. When they are not, other rules apply).

Category 1: Scale lines that descend for chords that last two beats each,

Category 2: Scale lines that ascend for chords that last two beats each,

Category 3: Scales lines that ascend and descend for chords that last four beats each, or longer.

Descending Scale Lines That Last For Chords Two Beats Each

In example #1, the scale of C7, which is common to G-7, C7, Fmaj. in the key of " F," has been reordered into seven, descending four-note scale groups.

Example 1:

These groupings have been selected and reordered by synchronizing each grouping's last notes to fall on 1 & 3 of the bar spelling out each chord as in Examples #2 – 2B.

Example 2:

Example 2A:

Example 2B:

In Examples 3 – 3B the same process has been applied to the II-V-I in the relative minor key of D-: E-7b5, A7#9, D-.

Example 3:

Example 3A:

Example 3B:

In Examples #4 – 4C, the four groupings selected from Example #2 that end on the roots, 3rds, 5ths, and 7ths of G-7 (G, Bb, D, F), C7 (C, E, G, Bb), and Fmaj (F, A, C, E), become reordered once again, back into consecutive scales, but rearranged to spell out the changes II-V-I in the key of Fmaj. The same can be done with the relative minor II-V-I as well.

Example 4:

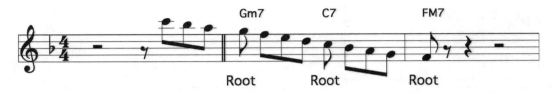

Example 4A:

Example 4B:

Example 4C:

As the chord-tones progress in a predictable manner (all roots, all 3rds, all 5ths, all 7ths), the soloist begins to acquire the "sense" of the logic inherent in the progression of changes and their chord-tones to the degree that one can hear where they are going over longer and longer distances.

CHAPTER 3

Once this ability has been established, the chord-tones you wish to approach can be mixed in almost any manner, as in Example #5.

Example 5:

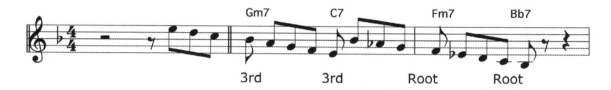

The following is a list of some the combinations of chord-tones that are possible on II-V-I's in any key.

1-1-1/1-1-3/1-1-5/1-1-7/1-3-1/1-5-1/1-7-1/3-1-1/3-3-1/3-5-1/3-7-1/ 5-1-1/5-3-1/7-3-1/7-1-1/7-3-1/7-5-1/1-3-3/1-3-5/1-3-7/1-5-3/ 1-5-5/1-5-7/1-7-1/1-7-3/1-7-5/1-7-7/3-3-3/5-5-5/7-7-7/3-3-1/ 3-3-5/3-3-7/5-5-1/5-3-1/5-7-1/7-7-1/7-5-1/7-3-1-/ etc., etc.

Not including octave adjustment, there are over 75 possible combinations of 1/3/5/7 on a II-V-I progression. Although all of the possibilities don't sound good, the number of ways in which virtually any sequence of chords can be spelled out using these four- note groups are almost infinite, clearly demonstrating that discipline and freedom are not inconsistent concepts.

Example #6 shows descending four-note groups going to all thirds on a cycle of Dom 7ths and how they can be octave adjusted to create even more melodic possibilities. Note that they become common bebop scale lines.

Example 6:

In the case of ascending scale lines, the soloist may not be able to approach the chord tones of each chord without adding half-steps to synchronize the line. However, any scale line, ascending or descending, of any length, over a II-V or II-V-I, will sound strong if the last note of the line is a basic chord-tone of the last chord (the approached chord) of a sequence. For example:

Example 7:

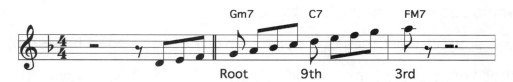

As in the above example, the ability to hear toward tension tones of a scale may be developed, creating a richer scale sound.

There is a difference between practicing and performance and the goals of each are different. When practicing these exercises, the goal is to achieve a planned result: to train your ear to hear towards certain points in the future. When in a playing context the goal is the opposite; to achieve the unplanned result of be able to start on any note and any

CHAPTER 3

beat and hear where your line is resolving to. The following *Forward Motion* exercises are multi-purpose.

This is an interesting way for beginners to practice learning their scales. They sound more like how they sound in performance. Because you're using your ear to practice, rather than the intellect, they are easier to learn.

For more advanced students, who know their scales, these exercises function to re-train the way you have previously heard scales into hearing with FM. They are only to be used as a starting point. As soon as you have begun to change your hearing, go to the following exercises to learn how to synchronize them to spell out chord scales. Your goal is to gain the ability to start a line on any beat of the bar and hear it going to its up-coming resolution point, the target note and beat.

The next subject discusses one particular use of the added half-step, the one that keeps scale tension and release patterns in synch with the rhythmic tension and release patterns of the bar.

Ascending Scale Lines for Chords that Last Two Beats Each

The Target Notes in ascending lines are treated differently as they move in cycles of 5ths.

This section is an introduction to what may be termed the "Added Optional Corrective Half-step." It is not intended as a complete discussion of the subject of *Forward Motion* and Chromatics as discussed in Chapter Five. Depending where in a scale or bar you begin your scale line, it may be necessary to add a half-step to correct a line when you sense that a scale melody will be going "out of synch," reaching a target note too soon or too late. It is optional because it used only when needed. However, you won't know whether to add the half-step unless you are hearing your target notes in advance.

The added half-step keeps scale tension and release patterns in synch with the rhythmic tension and release patterns of the bar. The added half-step is also applied to the second and third categories of scale lines: scale lines that ascend for two beats for chord changes that last for two beats each and, ascending and descending scale lines that last for four beats per change and longer.

The chromatic is a much-abused interval. The old adage that "if the note you played is wrong, the right one is either a half-step above or below" is an often misused improvisational device that creates weak

CHAPTER 3

melodies. This section offers certain "rules" for practicing adding a half-step in the "right" place to keep scale lines "in synch." One can't really improvise using rules.

RULE 1:

A half-step may be added at any point in a scale where the interval of a whole-tone exists. All seven-note scales have five whole-step intervals to which a half-step may be added to correct a melodic line, depending on which note and beat you start your line on.

RULE 2:

When approaching basic chord tones, scale-wise from below, a half-step may be added so that the Target Notes of the four-note groups end on the root, 3rd, 5th, and 7th of the chord being spelled out on "1" and "3" of the bar.

RULE 3:

Any basic chord tone may be approached from below by an added half-step. Where a half-step approach already exists below a chord tone, a half-step may be added in the whole-step interval just below it.

In Examples #9-11, the four note groups that spell out the Roots, 3rds, 5ths and 7ths of G-7, C7 and, Fmaj.7 have been selected and the half-steps added according to the above rules.

Example 9:

Example 10:

Example 11:

Examples #12-15 show these groups reordered into ascending scale lines with all the Roots, 3rds, 5ths and 7ths Synchronized to spell out II-V-I.

Example 12: All Roots

CHAPTER 3

Example 13: All Thirds

Example 14: All Fifths

Example 15: All Sevenths

Apply the added half-step process to the II-V-1's in the relative minor keys as well.

As an experiment, try adding the half-step into any other of the whole-step intervals and you'll notice the stark difference between lines that are in and out of synch. How to add half-steps to the other whole-step intervals in a scale will be demonstrated later in this chapter.

Create more interesting lines by applying octave adjustments and the almost infinite possible choices of Target Note combinations, such as in Examples #16-17.

Example 16:

Example 17:

Example #18 shows how ascending and descending scale lines may be mixed on a common set of chord changes.

Example 18:

Example #19 is on the changes to the first four bars of one of the most played standards in American music.

Example 19:

Example #21 shows Example #19 with the inner guide-tone melody isolated from the 8th note line. You'll see that scale lines that last for chord changes that are four beats per change now contain two basic chord-tones of each chord within a bar. This is the third category of scale lines in action.

Example 21:

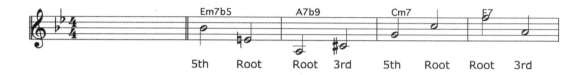

At this point the soloist transcends the mere playing of "Key Scales" into playing "Chord Scales;" i.e., scales that are common to their diatonic chords, that when reordered and the half-step added where needed, can spell out these chords.

Ascending and Descending Scale Lines for Chords that Last Four or More Beats Each

Scalar rhythmic tension and release patterns occur in pairs. Chord Scale tension and release patterns also occur in a duple manner, except at one point in every seven-note scale where two chord tones are neighbors (a whole-step apart.) At this point the duple scale tension and release patterns reverse, becoming "out of synch" with the duple rhythmic tension and release patterns. A half-step may be added between these two chord tones to keep the rhythmic and melodic tension and release patterns "in synch."

RULE 4:

A half-step may be added between the 5th and the 6th tones of the scale on all major and minor 6th (Maj. 7th) chord scales (the "one" chord of a major or minor key); In general, the added half-step will be on an "off" the beat.

RULE 5:

A half-step may be added between the flat 7th and the Root on all chord scales with a flat 7th (Dom7th, Min7th Min7thb5). Examples #22- 28 show the seven diatonic scales in the key of "C" with the added half-steps between the neighbor chord tones.

Example 22:

Example 23:

Example 24:

CHAPTER 3

Example 25:

Example 26:

Example 27:

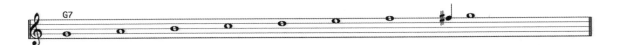

Example 28:

Example 29:

The rhythmic and melodic tension and release patterns of these diatonic scales can now be synchronized to create *Forward Motion* exercises.

Example 30:

Example 31:

Example 31a:

Example 32:

Example 33:

CHAPTER 3

Example 34:

Example 35:

Notice how the chord tones are synchronized with the "on" beats of the bars.

The above exercises show the groupings going to alternating Roots and 5ths. They may also be practiced going to target notes of alternating 3rds and 7ths (or 6ths). Transpose these exercises into all twelve keys.

Every possibility of every concept can't be practiced. There isn't enough time in life to do so and it's not necessary anyway. When do you stop practicing *Forward Motion*? When you've practiced it enough to get it in your ears so that everything you play is in FM. When is enough? Your ears will tell you. Graduate to practicing transcribed solos of your favorite players. Make sure you're copying using FM Notation as well. Circle the notes on "1" and "3" of the bars, isolate the inner guide tone melodies and practice those before you try to play the complete melodic line. Always use this process when practicing anything.

Adding Additional Half-steps to a Scale

Examination of common usage reveals that half-steps are often added not only between the whole tone interval between flat 7th and 1 of a 7th chord and the 5th and 6th of a major or minor 6th chord but any other whole-step interval in a scale as well. Every seven-note scale contains five whole-step intervals where a half-step may be added. To maintain the concept of "spelling" out chord changes, i.e., synchronizing the chord tones with "on" beats, any additional half-steps should be placed on "off" beats as in the following examples. However, adding additional half-steps may throw a scale line "out of synch" at a later place in the scale line and might need to be corrected by adding one or more additional half-steps. Where you add these half-steps depends on what note and beat of the bar you begin your scale line on and which beat and note you plan to end upon.

CHAPTER 3

Descending Scale Lines With Added Half-steps

Example 37:

Example 38:

Example 39:

Example 40:

Example 41:

Example 42:

Example 43:

Example 44:

Examples 43 and 44 are examples of "Superimposed" scales. If we read the notes that fall on the first and third beats of the bars as chord tones the 2nd bar spells out C7 and the first half of the 3rd bar spells out G-7. Superimposition will be discussed in greater detail in Chapter 9.

Example 45:

Ascending Scale Lines With Added Half-steps

Example 46:

Example 47:

Example 48:

Example 49:

Example 50:

Create exercises adding notes to the relative II-V's in a minor key as well.

Create exercises combining various ascending and descending scale lines.

When and where to add the additional half-steps varies according to when and where you start and intend to resolve your line. It can't be done by rules. These additions can be successfully accomplished only if you're hearing ahead towards your last note and sense that you're going to arrive at your target note and beat either too early or late. Start ascending and descending scale lines on any off beat, on any added half-step to test if you can hear where the added notes need to be placed to keep your line in sync.

ARPEGGIOS & *FORWARD MOTION*

Most students feel a strong gravitational pull toward arpeggios since they spell out chord changes when aligned with a chord's basic chord tones. The synchronization of arpeggiated chord tones with resolution beats is easier to accomplish than with scalar lines. Scale lines tend to inherently have more potential for resolution than arpeggios. Consequently, applying FM to arpeggios may require alteration by placing them differently in the bar or adding pick-ups and/or resolutions tones to them.

Unresolved and Resolved Arpeggios

Arpeggios come in two types; Unresolved and Resolved. Both types are in common usage in the history of jazz vocabulary.

Melodic Inversions:

An integral component of practicing any melodic theme, scales, chromatics, intervals and arpeggios, is Melodic Inversion. Applying Melodic inversion to any exercise insures you have practiced all the possible ways themes can be used to create "shapes," or rapid and interesting changes in direction.

When practicing themes always play every inversion. Not so much for theme memorization but to internalize **the process** of Melodic Inversion. Write out, in one key, all four inversions of the theme you're working on and do the 12-key work transposing from the written example. Once you become familiar with the process you won't need the paper any more. At that point you will have the process internalized and you'll be able to intuitively apply the process to your improvisations.

There are four inversions of every exercise:

The notes within the groupings ascend and the groupings ascend:

Example 1:

The notes within the groupings descend and the groupings ascend.

Example 2:

The notes within the groupings ascend and the groupings descend.

CHAPTER 4

Example 3:

The notes within the groupings descend and the groupings descend.

Example 4:

"Shape-making" occurs when you mix the various inversions. The following mixed inversions are alternating but can be mixed in any manner.

Example 5:

Example 6:

Example 7:

Example 8:

Arpeggios in thirds can be played and combined in groups of 2s, 3s, 4s, 5s, 6s, and 7s (Example 9) in all inversions. As this book is not meant to be a discussion of the theory of improvisation in thirds, experimentation combining various size arpeggios and melodic inversions are left up to the student's imagination.

Example 9:

Example 9a:

Example 9b:

Example 9c:

Example 9d:

Unresolved Arpeggios

The preceding examples of arpeggios in thirds have no resolution nor do they sound like pick-ups as they stand. To create *Forward Motion* for unresolved arpeggios, they need to be adjusted in relation to the bar lines. For example:

Example 10:

Example 11:

Example 11A

Example 11B:

Example 12:

CHAPTER 4

You should begin to notice the appearance of one of the most important aspects of FM processes; **when FM is applied to a theme, it becomes transformed into another melody. This is the true melody**. Examples of this will appear with greater frequency as you develop your ability to translate exercises into FM. Until we arrived at example # 10, the preceding examples were only exercises and not true melodic content. They were "static" and had no motion.

The following is a tetra chord mixed inversions exercise (Example #9, second line) that segues into the subject of arpeggios with pick-ups and resolutions. You'll notice its transformation into a different melody immediately.

First, the example without the application of FM:

Example 13:

The exercise with FM applied.

Example 14:

The notes proceed in the same order but now the exercise is transformed into a completely different sounding melodic theme. What at first was ascending groups of four-note stacks of thirds is now three note triads with added ascending scale step resolutions on "1" & "3" of the bars.

The Inner Guide-Tone Melody in this case is:

Example 15:

Resolving Arpeggios and Creating Pick-ups

Create resolved arpeggios by adding an ascending or descending scale step at its end. The resolution note should be on "1" and/or "3' of the bar.

Create pick-ups by adding a scale or half-step approach, from either above or below, to the first note of the arpeggio. The added pick-up should be on an off-beat, an "and." Examples 12 and 14 show how this can some times be achieved without adding any pick-ups and resolutions, by just changing the beat on which the theme begins. This is not always the case. Some exercises require the addition of a note to create FM.

CHAPTER 4

The following is a commonly found melodic fragment in the jazz vocabulary:

Example 16:

The example is not notated in FM and may give a false impression of the true melodic line. It may be given two interpretations when translated into FM notation.

Example 17:

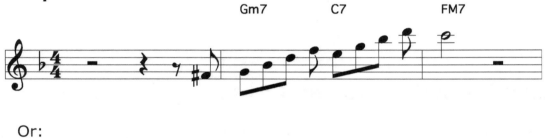

Or:

Example 18:

Each example demonstrates two slightly different ways the line may be heard internally. The examples begin with an added half-step pick up from below, to the root of the G-7, then a descending scale step resolution from the flat 7th of the G-7, ending with another scale step resolution moving down to the 5th of the F major chord

Here's another example of resolutions and pick-ups commonly found the jazz vocabulary.

Example 19: (Without FM notation)

Example 20:

Or

Example 21:

The example starts with an ascending half-step scale pick up to the 3rd of the G-7. The 9th of the G-7 then resolves downward to the flat 13th of the C7 with the flat 7th resolving down to the 3rd of the F major chord.

CHAPTER 4

Another commonly used technique to create FM with an arpeggio is to consider the last two notes as a double, scale-wise appoggiatura from above and below, bracketing the 1st note of a scale line. (More on appoggiaturas in the next chapter).

Example 22:

Example 23:

Or

Example 23a:

Internally each version is heard differently. This is one of the goals of FM, **to gain the ability to switch they way you hear a line internally at will**. When each version begins to sounds differently in the ear, each version will then be phrased differently. How you perceive a played or written phrase internally affects the way it is articulated externally.

Scale and arpeggiated lines can be combined. Applying FM to these combinations have been hinted at in some of the preceding examples. However, a few more examples will suffice in clarifying the issue.

Example 24:

Example 24a:

Example 26:

CHAPTER 4

Example 27:

The examples in this chapter demonstrate only a few of the possible ways arpeggios may be played. Experiment breaking up and combining the arpeggios into different shapes. Arpeggios and scales can be combined in limitless ways. Experiment using them in different combinations. By this time you should be familiar enough with the concept of FM to be able to hear whether you're applying the concept or not.

FORWARD MOTION
AND APPOGGIATURAS

Appoggiaturas spell out chord changes because they embellish chord tones. Called "filigrees" in the jazz vernacular, along with arpeggiation, they were one of the most commonly used devices of early jazz improvisation. Jazz improvisers have historically tended to show a desire to play outside of the key. Chromatic appoggiaturas fulfilled this desire.

They can occur on any beat of the bar but often show up being played on the "on" or release beats. Even though they might start on the beat, because of their generally chromatic nature, they have a tendency to make release beats and chord tones more tense, giving them a feeling of *Forward Motion*.

When I was a student at Berklee School of Music (as it was called when I attended), the list of appoggiaturas we were given were endless. Each had its own rather complex name. For clarity's sake, they are avoided here. As this book is not intended to be a theory or exercise book per se, only an abbreviated list will be included and will be restricted to the most commonly used versions. Once you get the idea of how appoggiaturas are constructed, you should be able to add to the list with a little experimentation.

Appoggiaturas can be simple or complex. Each has its "mirror" versions. The more complex, the more mirror versions there are. As always, it's best to start with the simple and move toward the complex. FM will be applied to all examples. The C triad will be used throughout. The student is left to their own devices in applying them to other chord qualities such as minor, diminished, and whole tone triads and 7th chords

Example 1: 1/2 step below (the chord tone) to the chord tone

Example 1a shows the Dizzy's composition "The Champ" with appoggiaturas being used with the non-chord tones of a Bb diminished chord "on" the beat. This tends to make the "on" beats tense or give them a swing impetus.

Example 1a:

Example 2: 1/2 step above to the chord tone

Example 3: 1 whole-step below to the chord tone

Example 4: 1 whole-step above to the chord tone:

Example 5: 1 whole-step below to 1/2 step below to the chord tone

Example 6: 1 whole-step above to 1/2 step above to the chord tone

CHAPTER 5

Example 7: 1/2 step below to 1/2 step above to the chord tone

Example 8: 1/2 step above to 1/2 step below to the chord tone

Example 9: 1 whole-step below to 1 whole-step above to the chord tone

Example 10: 1 whole-step above to 1 whole-step below to the chord tone

Example 11: 1/2 step below to 1 whole-step above to a 1/2 step above to the chord tone

Example 12: 1/2 step above to 1 whole-step below to a 1/2 step below to the chord tone

Example 13: 1 Whole-step below to 1/2 step below to 1 whole-step above to 1/2 step above to the chord tone: Because of limitations of space the following examples are for ascending appoggiatura groups only. At this point you should have the idea of how to construct the descending groups on your own.

CHAPTER 5

Example 14: 1 Whole-step above to 1/2 step above to 1 whole-step below to 1/2 step below to the chord tone

The following examples start on the chord tone, on the beat.

Example 15: chord tone, to 1/2 step above to the chord tone

Example 16: chord tone, to 1/2 step below to the chord tone

The approaches from above and below can be applied to whole-step approaches as well.

Example 17: chord tone to 1/2 step above, to 1/2 step below, to chord tone

Example 18: its mirror version: chord tone to 1/2 step below, to 1/2 step above, to chord tone

The approaches from above and below can be applied to whole and/ or 1/2 step approaches and their mirror versions.

Example 19: Chord tone, to 1/2 step above to chord tone to 1/2 step below, to chord tone. Triplitising the "on" beats gives the "on" beats a feeling of tension or swing

You should have a firm idea of how various appoggiaturas are constructed. Test yourself by finding the mirror versions of examples from some of the preceding examples.

An often used appoggiatura in the jazz vocabulary is the triple chromatic from above and the triple chromatic from below.

CHAPTER 5

Example 20:

Example 21:

The list goes on and on from here. Experiment with various combinations and study their usage in the jazz vocabulary. Many musicians can be identified by the appoggiaturas they've selected as part of their vocabulary.

INTERVALS AND *FORWARD MOTION*

Intervals larger than a third require the same adjustments as arpeggios as in themselves they have no resolution. Large intervals can start on or off the beat. Melodic intervals are usually what are termed "broken arpeggios" created by skipping notes in an arpeggio. Skipping alternating notes as in the C7 chord below we come up with the following intervals notated as pick ups. As in previous chapters, for the sake of thouroughness, the examples are written in exercise format. In performance selected intervals are used as components of melodic lines.

Example 1:

Example 2:

CHAPTER 6

Example 2a:

Skipping two notes in the arpeggio gives the following intervals:

Example 3:

Example 3a:

Skipping every other note results in the following intervals of a Bbmaj.

7th chord looks like this:

Example 5:

Example 5a:

Skipping every two notes:

Example 6:

Intervals may be used in an unresolved manner but tend to become super melodic when combined with scale step pick-ups and resolutions from above and/or below the first and/or last notes. Tin Pan Alley tune-smiths frequently used intervals in many of the classic American standard songs. For example:

Branislaw Kaper's "Invitation"

Example 7:

Victor Young's "Be My Love"

Example 8:

CHAPTER 6

Cole Porter's "I Love You"

Example 9:

In every case, where used, the pick-ups create FM and the resolutions create a resolution where none existed in the interval itself.

Examples of intervallic FM are frequently found in jazz compositions such as in Charlie Parker's "Milestones" and Monk's "Mysterioso."

Example 10:

Example 11:

Large intervals are common in the jazz improvisers vocabulary. The following are a few Db diminished chord or C7b9 intervallic exercises I remember practicing in my youth

Example 12:

Example 12a: (using FM notation)

Example 13:

Example 14:

Example 15:

Can you mentally translate examples 14 and 15 into FM notation?

This ability will develop as you practice more exercises with FM.

CHAPTER 6

The following examples demonstrate how intervals, pick-ups and resolution notes might be used in a solo.

Example 16:

One more example of common intervallic usage:

Example 17:

In the example above we have in the second bar a double chromatic approach (appoggiatura) from below going up to the 3rd of the C7 then an interval up to what appears to be the 9th of the C7. In FM Analysis however, the descending scale line would be considered a Harmonic FM scale line spelling out the FM7 a beat and a half before the chord arrives on "one" of the last bar. Harmonic FM will be discussed in greater detail in Chapter 7.

HARMONIC *FORWARD MOTION*

The most sophisticated form of FM is Harmonic *Forward Motion* wherein chord changes are spelled out ahead of where they are written on the paper. Becoming a lost art, HFM can only be implemented after having played your own vocabulary for many years. Allegedly, Bird could spell out changes two bars in advance of where they were written. He used to turn piano players around. They'd think he'd dropped a couple of bars, and like any good accompanist, would go with him. Bird would tell them, "Don't come with me. Stay where you are. When you hit the chord change, it will resolve the tension created by my spelling the change ahead of time."

HMF techniques can usually only be applied after the improviser has developed complete familiarity and control of their vocabulary. Two present day players that have a firm grasp of HFM are James Moody and Jerry Bergonzi.

In an effort to introduce students to the concept, I've included beat-and-a-half HFM in most of the exercises in this book. Perhaps a schematic will explain better than words can.

When most students see a set of chord changes, such as a II-V-I they

CHAPTER 7

assume that the melodic lines (the brackets) are played within the bar, where the chord symbols are written.

Example 1:

However, these FM exercises spell out the changes one beat and a half ahead of where the chord symbols are written.

Example 2:

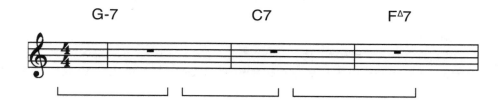

Mistakes in transcriptional analysis often occur because lines are analyzed in terms of the chord symbol as opposed to the more accurate method of analyzing in terms of what the line itself is spelling out by the placement of its notes on"1" and "3" of the bar or on every quarter-note.

For example, in Chapter 3 (*Scalar Forward Motion*), example 3 demonstrated the use of mixed Target Notes.

Example 3:

Normal transcriptional analysis would define the Ab in the second bar as the flat 13th of the C7 chord Analyzed using HMF would define this note as the flat 7th of the Bb 7th being spelled out three beats and a half in advance of the Bb7 change in the next bar.

. . . . . Barry Harris once related to me one of the techniques used to apply HFM. He said: "Oh Hal, in bebop we don't play the II-7 chord," as in the second descending scale line in example 3 which plays the Bb7 scale while the F-7 chord is being played. Playing the V 7 while the II-7 change is occurring spells out the V7 ahead of time.

In examples 4 – 7 the same melodic line is moved increasingly farther ahead of the upcoming changes.

Example 4:

CHAPTER 7

Example 5:

Example 6:

Example 7:

How good example 7 would sound depends on how the line was resolved as in example 7a.

Example 7a:

The same melodic line can also be delayed, starting at later points in the bar yet still be in FM

Example 7b:

Example 7c:

The line still sounds good but needs to be resolved to the FM7 on the last beat in the last bar as in the next example.

Example 7d:

Another HFM technique is to use common notes between the change you're playing and the change you're going to as in example 8.

CHAPTER 7

Example 8:

In this case the last grouping of each bar has common tones with the upcoming change. The following example demonstrates mixed usage of common tones.

Example 9:

Example 10: shows how changes can be anticipated a bar in advance.

Example 11: is an excerpt from a Coltrane middle period solo where he spells out descending II-V's ahead of the changes

An improviser's ultimate goal is to achieve rhythmic, melodic and harmonic freedom to place any melodic line anywhere, at any point in a bar, and still have it sound good.

PENTATONICS & CELLS WITH *FORWARD MOTION*

In this chapter Pentatonic and Cell improvising are discussed only in terms of how *Forward Motion* affects these concepts. Because of the limitations of space and a commitment to stay focused on the discussion at hand a more complete theory of both best be left to a later book on these subjects.

Pentatonic Scales With FM

All the examples in this chapter will, for demonstration purposes, use the most basic pentatonic scale: 1, 2, 3, 5, 6, of the major scale, with the understanding that FM concepts can be applied to the other thirty-seven pentatonic scales as well.

Example 1: the demonstration scale

There are five modes to each pentatonic scale that can be organized into five consecutive four-note scale groups. Examples 2-5 shows them, without FM, in all four Melodic Inversions.

Example 2:

Example 3:

Example 4:

Example 4a:

The following examples demonstrate examples 2 - 4 in FM.

Example 5:

Example 6:

Although no two musicians hear the same way, it sounds like the three groupings in the preceding examples that begin with a scale step pick-up have more FM than the two groupings that begin with scale 3rd pick-ups. You will observe that, as we progress through the chapter, this can change depending upon which pick ups you're using at the moment and whether the grouping(s) descend or ascend.

Example 7:

Every melodic fragment has its Inner Guide Tone melody. In this case:

Example 7a:

Defining Inner Guide Tone Melodies may be applied universally to any melody. Look for them in every exercise. Although it will be discussed again in the chapter on How To Practice FM, it is worth reiterating.

Example 8:

Example 9: an example of mixed Melodic Inversions

Example 10: In FM

Example 11: The Inner Guide Tone Melody

Examples 12-12c demonstrate the previous groupings with a beat pick-up.

CHAPTER 8

Example 12:

Example 12a:

Example 12b:

Example 12c:

As above, apply Melodic Inversions to every example then define its Inner Guide Tone.

Examples 13 - 13c illustrates example 12 with alternating Melodic Inversions.

Example 13:

Example 13a:

Example 13b:

Example 13c:

Define the Inner Guide Tone Melody for these examples.

Examples 14-17 demonstrate the same groupings with a half-beat pick-up.

Example 14:

Example 15:

Example 16:

CHAPTER 8

Example 17:

Apply alternating Melodic Inversions to the preceding examples.

Pentatonic melodic fragments can be connected in infinite ways, one of the most common being Intervallic Root Motion. Groups can ascend in half-steps as the first mode does in example 18.

Example 18:

Most exercise books print their exercises in the manner above, without FM. One of the ways to convert them into FM is to leave out the first note and beat and start the exercise on the second note, second beat as in example 19 and mentally translate it into FM notation.

Example 19:

As you can see, the pattern when translated into FM, takes on a different shape. The pick-ups move toward the last note of each four-note fragment. The exercise although beginning within the bar, has more

FM to it. A more intense feeling of FM can be created by moving the exercise back to start on the "&" of beat three in the preceding bar.

Example 20:

The Inner Guide Tone Melody ascends in half-steps.

Example 21:

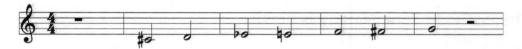

More interesting "shapes" are created when you apply alternating Melodic Inversions to example 18.

Example 22:

Begin the exercise on the second beat and note and you get the following.

Example 23:

CHAPTER 8

Moving the exercise back to begin on the "&" of three in the preceding bar results in the following.

Example 24:

The Inner Guide Tone Melody is now:

Example 25:

Apply alternating Melodic Inversions to the above exercises and translate them into FM.

To create longer lines the modes may be "stacked" together as in the following examples.

Example 26:

Taking this exercise through the same steps as the preceding exercises results in the following.

Example 27:

Spelling Chord Changes with Pentatonics

"If you can't spell out changes with pentatonic groups you haven't gained complete control over them." **Woody Shaw**

It was mentioned in an earlier chapter that strong melodies "spell out" chord changes. Applying FM to spell out changes using pentatonic groupings uses the same process as in the chapter on Scalar FM. It is the nature of pentatonics that they are weaker than the seven and eight note scales as they contain less basic chord tones. This weakness is also an advantage. Although they tend to spell out the chords with a little less accuracy than 7 and 8-note scales, they can be superimposed over the changes with much more freedom.

Pentatonics tend to be used mostly in modal playing but can be applied to change playing as well. Mr. Shaw's advice suggests that there are two categories of pentatonic lines: those that spell out changes, "Basic" pentatonic lines, and the more free floating lines such as are played in modal, " Superimposed" melodic lines. Superimposition will be discussed at greater length chapter 9.

The chord tones 3rd, flat 3rd, and the flat 7th spell out the character and color of changes with the greatest clarity. Every grouping may not contain both of these basic chord tones but will contain at least one of them. If the chord tone(s) is aligned with '1" and/or "3" of the bar it will not so much spell out the change as "suggest" it.

Of the 38 pentatonic scales, a number of them can be used to spell out basic changes.

Example 28: Spells out Cmaj6 and A-7

Example 29: Spells out C7

Example 30: the 5th mode of the Eb pentatonic scale spells out C-7

Example 31: the 3rd mode of the Ab7th pentatonic scale spells out C-7b5

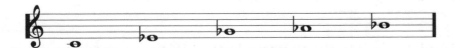

Example 32: Spells out C7b9 or Db Diminished

Example 33: Spells out C7 Altered

Pentatonic scales spell out every chord quality common to the jazz harmonic vocabulary but we'll confine this discussion to applying pentatonics to II-V's and II-V-Is.

All five modes of each scale can be used on its designated chord quality but some modes contain more basic chord tones than others. Example 34 shows the five modes of the G-7 scale. Three of the groups have three of the G-7 chord tones and the remaining two have only two.

CHAPTER 8

The more chord tones in a grouping there are the more it spells out a change.

Example 34:

The C7 pentatonic scale has three groupings with three chord tones in them, one grouping with four chord tones and one grouping with two:

Example 35:

The FM6 pentatonic has three groupings with three chord tones one grouping with four chord tones and one grouping with 2 chord tones in them:

Example 36:

Selecting the strongest groupings to spell out II-Vs results in the following.

Example 37:

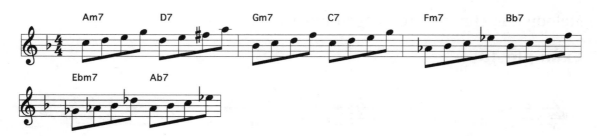

As in all other examples, number 37 can be translated into FM. Of the three possible pick-ups, in this case, the pick-up on "four' of the preceding bar sounds good. Which pick-up can be used varies on a case-by-case basis according to which of the five modes you've selected.

Example 38:

The Inner Guide Tone Melody in example 38 is alternating 5ths and 3rds

Example 39:

CHAPTER 8

Example 40 now has a beat and a half pick-up. The Inner Guide Tone Melody has changed to alternating flat 7ths and 3rds

Example 40:

Example 41 uses the same groupings but in alternating Melodic Inversions.

Example 41:

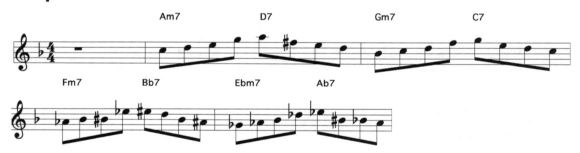

The above example in FM now becomes:

Example 42:

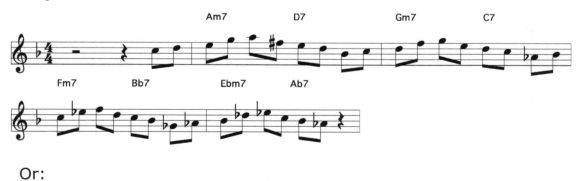

Or:

Example 43:

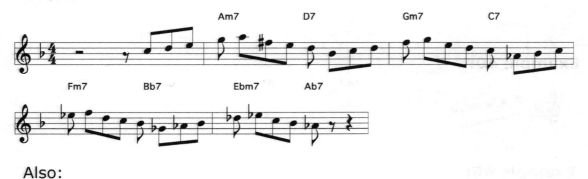

Also:

Example 44:

Example 44 bears examining in terms of how the Inner Guide Tone Melody falls on the 1st and 3rd beats of the bar. Even though the 1st grouping of each pair is from the minor 7th chord, it sounds like the dominant all the way through each pair. That's because the root of the dominant is on the 1st beat and the 3rd of the dominant on the 3rd beat, emphasizing the dominant sound. This is another example of Harmonic FM.

The preceding examples were all on chord changes that lasted for two beats each. The following ones are for chords that last for a bar each and use two groupings from each pentatonic scale.

CHAPTER 8

Example 45:

Example 46:

Example 47:

Example 48:

This same process can be applied to all chord qualities. Experiment

with the various groupings and Melodic Inversions. Always define the

Inner Chord Tone Guide Melody before attempting to practice the complete line.

The following example illustrates of how the process of FM works in modal situation.

Example 49:

Pentatonic arpeggios are treated in the same manner as are the arpeggios in chapter four. They are arrived at by skipping every other note, can be broken into two to five note arpeggios, and combined in any manner.

Except for double, triple and quadruple chromatic approaches from above, appoggiaturas of the kind in chapter five are rarely used in pentatonic playing. One of the dominant stylistic aspects of pentatonic improvisation is its almost complete lack of chromaticism. For that reason chromatics are not discussed in this chapter.

CHAPTER 8

Cell Improvising & *Forward Motion*

Cell Improvising is a recent development that offers an alternate and simplified approach toward improvising. The concept was derived from pentatonic improvising. Evidence of this concept exists before the advent of pentatonic improvising, most notably in Coltrane's "middle period" before he began his explorations into pentatonic playing. Additional evidence of Cell Improvising's beginnings can also be found in the solos of Freddy Hubbard and Junior Cook. One of the foremost practitioners of this concept is Jerry Bergonzi.

The concept is founded on the principle that the strongest four-note groups are those that contain three chord tones and one non-chord tone. The only stronger four-note-group is the arpeggio containing the four basic chord tones root, 3rd, 5th, and 7th However, one can't improvise using solely arpeggios. The strength of these groupings allows the improviser to spell out changes, both basic and superimposed, using a minimal amount of improvisational information: the triad with an added note and a four-note consecutive scale group.

There are four types of triads: major, minor, diminished and whole tone in their root, 2nd, and 3rd inversions

Example 50: The major triad

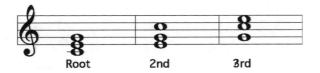

Example 51: The minor triad

Example 52: The diminished triad

Example 53: The whole tone triad

An added whole or half-step may inserted before the first note, between the first and second note, between the second and third note and after the third note. The following examples are shown only using scale step additions. Extrapolate the concept to the other triads. Try them with an added chromatic as well. The possibilities are almost limitless.

CHAPTER 8

Example 54: The major triad

Example 55: The minor triad

Example 56: The diminished triad

Example 57: The whole tone triad

This results in the following four note groups.

Example 58: Root Inversion

Example 59: 2ⁿᵈ Inversion

Example 60: 3ʳᵈ Inversion

These added notes were inserted in the first Melodic Inversion. Apply the process to the other three Melodic Inversions.

Cell playing for scale groups introduces an alternate way to perceive four note scale groupings than was discussed in the chapter on Scalar *Forward Motion*. To simplify the concept we'll analyze these groups looking for those with three chord tones and one non-chord tone. They're usually flat 7th chords of one kind or another.

Example 61:

Analyzing each cell individually illustrates that each has three chord tones and one non-chord tone.

Example 62: the three chord tones in the group are 5th, flat 7th, and root of G7

Example 63: has three chord tones: flat 7, root and flat 3rd of D-7

Example 64: has the 5th, flat 7th, and root of an A-7 chord

Example 65: has the flat 7th, root, and flat 3rd of a G-7

Example 66 has either the flat 7th, root, and flat 3rd of an A-7 (shown) or the 5th, flat 7th, and root of a C7. It makes no difference how you name it as it still has three chord tones and one non-chord tone.

Example 66:

Example 67: has the 5th, flat 7th, and root of a D-7

Example 68: has the flat 7th, root, and 3rd of a C7

The following is a partial list of cells that start on each scale tone of a C7 scale.

Chapter 8

Example 69:

At this point you should have a firm enough sense of how FM works to apply the process to cells. They will all not start on the same beat. Some sound fine starting on the beat. Others sound better starting on the "&" of beat four, or beat four or the "&" of beat three. Experiment with various starting points to see which beats are appropriate for each cell. There also may be more than one particular starting point that would sound good on a cell.

Rather than demonstrate the various FM applications for each cell, example 70 illustrates how they might be used in a chorus of blues changes followed by an edited version. Pay particular attention to the phrase markings. The way you hear the phrases internally will come out externally in your playing. If you hear them as separate four-note groups they will come out sounding that way. Note that the phrase marks start ahead of the bar line crossing over the bar line to end in the middle of the next bar. Not only do the notes have to be in FM but the phrasing as well.

Example 70:

Example 71:

Note that the edited version has no changes written above the staff. The cell groups are so strong, they spell out the basic changes so clearly, that their passage can be heard without any chords being played behind in the background. We will return to the subject of Cell Improvising again in the next chapter on Superimposition.

CHAPTER 8

Cells come in infinite forms, however, our focus here is only on how FM affects cell playing. For a more complete discussion on cell playing read *Thesaurus of Intervallic Melodies Inside Improvisation, Vol. 5, by Jerry Bergonzi, (http://www.advancemusic.com).*

SUPERIMPOSITION

Premier bebop drummer Philly Joe Jones was once asked if he played "Free Music." "I've always played free," he responded. I can personally attest to his statement as I had the good fortune to have played with him a number of times.

What is the difference between "Free Music" and playing "Freely?" What Philly's questioner had in mind was the genre of jazz played by the likes of Ornette Coleman, Albert Ayler, their contemporaries and followers. What Philly had in mind was that one must be able to play "freely" in any musical genre. A somewhat surprising concept, that one can be "free" in such a reputedly conservative genre of jazz as bebop. The difference between the two concepts is that, in "Free Music" the organizing factors are less stringent than those of bebop. These organizing factors could be only a scale, or a melodic fragment, no set meter or just a single tone, almost anything. One could play more freely because of these minimalist organizing factors.

During my apprenticeship with Sam Rivers we'd often play tunes based on one root note. We'd play a tune on "E Anything." When thinking of what to play next the question was often "Okay, what note do you want to play on next?" The answer was often something like "let's play on F anything now."

CHAPTER 9

In bebop, to be authentic to the genre, the rhythmic, harmonic, and melodic organizing factors require being adhered to in a much more rigid fashion than "Free Music." This is not to suggest that playing "Free Music" is easier to play because there are less "rules" involved. Playing "Free Music" takes as much control and discipline as any other genre, just a different kind of discipline.

From my experience playing with Sam Rivers I learned that any music can be played freely, no matter the genre. Playing freely within a genre is often defined by those who can do it as "being able to play anything anywhere at any time and still make it sound good." To have internalized the predictable organizing factors, the "rules" if you will, to such degree that they need be used only as guides to keep your place in the tune. Dave Liebman wrote an excellent book on the subject of being able to "play anything anywhere" titled: *A Chromatic Approach To Jazz Harmony and Melody* (*Caris Music Services*, www.upbeat.com/caris)._

When I joined Cannonball Adderley's Quintet I was taken aside by their drummer and bassist and advised that I would have trouble being between the rhythm section and Cannonball because he "made up his own changes" whenever he felt like it. He had what I called "the courage of his line." If he felt or heard a melodic line going out of the tempo or outside the chord changes, he just went there. Luckily, because of my experience playing with Sam Rivers, I had no problem with this.

The crux of Superimposition is that **most of the great masters I I've played with made up their own changes over the original set.**

As long as your solo is confined to the original changes and tempo you're not free. Phil Woods has described it as "the tyranny of the tri-tone." The only way to achieve such freedom is through the use of superimposition.

The three components of music, rhythm, harmony and melody, can be superimposed over the original given set of rhythm, harmony and melody that make up a tune. The secret is how to do it and make it sound good. The reason anything sounds good is because the "rules' of music were applied properly. One aspect of musical rules is that they are operational until they're not. Then another set of rules becomes operational. There are always rules of one kind or another at work to make the music sound good.

Most of the preceding generations of masters learned the rules of jazz playing through the process of copying the music. It was not a requirement for these musicians to have taken a theory course in order to make their music sound good. The vocabulary taught it to them. The point being, you don't have to "know" the rules on an intellectual basis

CHAPTER 9

if you have learned them intuitively. There is a difference between being able to play anything anywhere and making mistakes. Making mistakes sounds bad because the rules that were in operation at the time were violated. Playing anything anywhere sounds good because the rules were observed.

Superimposition is different from the process known in jazz as "Substitution." Substitution changes the predetermined rhythmic, harmonic and melodic organizing factors of a tune. A G-7/C7 will be substituted, at a particular point in a tune by a Db-7/Gb7 and be played that way every time that part of the tune arrives.

Superimposition leaves the original set of organizing factors unchanged playing the superimposed ideas over or against them. A Db-7/ Gb7 could be superimposed **over** the G-7/C7 at any time the soloist feels like. A 4/4 tempo can be superimposed over a 3/4 tempo at any time the soloist feels like. The basic organizing factors of the tune's rhythm, harmony and melody content are used only as a reference point from which to depart and return and keep your place within the music.

The concept of Superimposition is based on an old, well-known compositional rule: **Any two musical ideas can go against each other as long as each of them has musical integrity.** In other words, as long as both ideas are strong ideas.

Forward Motion's focus is how to play musical ideas in the strongest possible ways. Superimposition is the path to musical freedom and the precepts of FM can be applied to all superimposed musical ideas.

Rhythmic Superimposition

Rhythmic sophistication is achieved by developing the ability to subdivide the beat into its smallest rhythmic increments with complete accuracy. Sonny Rollins is a master of rhythmic, harmonic and melodic superimposition. He can play anything anywhere.

Dizzy Gillespie was a guest with the Phil Woods Quintet for a week. At one point in every evening's performance I had to play a duo tune with Dizzy, his composition "Con Alma." As an accompanist it was a hair-raising experience. You could never predict where he was going to go next and he was a master super-imposer. He could go anywhere at any time and make it work. One day we were checking out of a hotel. We were both standing at the counter and I brought up the subject of rhythmic exercises. He mentioned a couple that he used to do when he was younger and I was amazed that we had created similar rhythmic exercises.

For example, in the following bar of 4/4 played with a 12/8 feeling.

CHAPTER 9

Example 1:

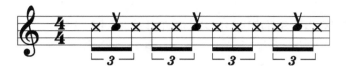

Trying to attack a note on any one of the above accented beats: the 2nd note of the first triplet, the 3rd note of the 2nd triplet or the 2nd note of the fourth triplet. The goal was to be able to repeatedly attack, with accuracy and control, singly or in any combination, any note of any of the triplets.

Superimposing a faster or slower tempo over the original tempo is another exercise that leads to rhythmic freedom. This is achieved by creating rhythm pyramids that subdivided the bar into even increments and playing the subdivision as another superimposed 4/4 tempo. Example 2 shows how a bar can be evenly subdivided into increasingly smaller rhythmic increments.

Example 2:

At any level of the pyramid a triplet may be introduced. In example 3 each quarter-note is divided into 8th note triplets. The triplets are then phrased in 4-note groups. This creates a slightly fast 4/4 tempo over the basic quarter-note tempo. These are called compound rhythms. The second stave is the quarter-note tempo.

Example 3:

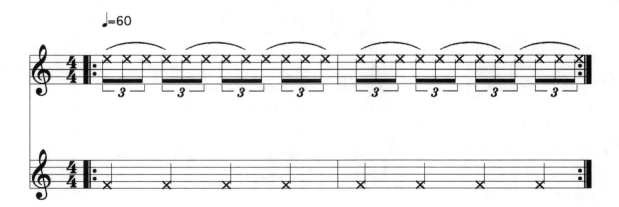

CHAPTER 9

Then add 4-note group bebop lines to the 8th note triplets, phrased in 4-note groups (see phrase marks). The resulting compound rhythm is 8th notes line played at a slightly faster 4/4 tempo superimposed over the basic 4/4 tempo.

Example 4:

The same process can be applied to 3/4 time as well.

Example 5:

At any level within the pyramid a duple rhythm may be divided by a triplet. At any level in the pyramid a triplet may be divided by a duple rhythm. Any of the compound rhythms in 3/4 can also be superimposed over any rhythmic levels of the duple pyramid creating more incrementally divided compound rhythms. Rhythm pyramids can be created in almost limitless configurations. Every time a cross rhythm is introduced into a pyramid the succeeding levels will be altered.

For the sake of clarity, and because of the limitations of notation programs, a compound rhythm will be created from the 4th level of the 3/4 pyramid by grouping the 8th notes into 4-note phrases.

Example 6:

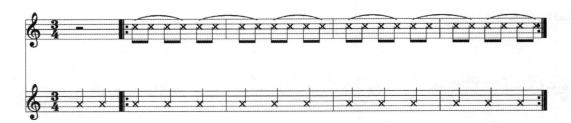

Example 7: illustrates the previous example with notes and FM phrasing added

CHAPTER 9

Compound tempos take conditioning to get comfortable with. This process can be applied to any rhythmic subdivision either metrical or "forced." (A "Forced" rhythm is one that is not evenly sub-dividable but stays constant within the tempo.)

Sam Rivers once quipped that "everything is in "C" and in 4/4." I didn't get it until I started working on these rhythmic exercises but what he meant was any odd meter can be played with a 4/4 phrasing. You just overlay your superimposed 4/4 rhythm over the tempo and correct the notes to fit the changes as they need be. This technique is often used to avoid playing everything in six-note phrases when soloing in 3/4. For example:

Example 8:

Compound tempos take practice. A shortcut for playing 4/4 phrasing on 3/4 is to tap 3/4 with one foot and tap every two beats with the right. The duple phrasing keeps turning over until it resolves on "one" of an upcoming bar. Then overlay 4/4, 8th note phrases over the 3/4 tempo.

The point being **superimposed rhythms and phrases have to be converted into *Forward Motion* phrasing.**

At this point the general concept of superimposition is hopefully clearer to the reader. The concept can also be applied to melodic improvising as well.

Melodic/Harmonic Superimposition

The term Melodic/Harmonic denotes that groups that are in FM are in actuality Melodic/Harmonic groupings that can stand alone from the chord changes they are played over.

Superimposition differs from ordinary change playing in that, in the accepted sense, extensions of a chord (the 9th, $\#9^{th}$, flat 9th, 11th, $\#11^{th}$, flat 5th and sharp $5^{th)}$ are named in terms of their distance from the root of a chord. This is a very cumbersome way of thinking. It is, for lack of a better word, "root-bound." Superimposition frees you from being "root-bound" °— considering these groupings as being independent of the basic changes forming strong melodic/harmonic themes within themselves, that have the ability to "float" over the basic changes, spelling out superimposed changes. The degree to which the player can tolerate the tension induced by this technique varies according to individual tastes.

Example 8a: illustrates this point

(The example sounds more consonant if the left hand voicing is played in an open 10th voicing: Root, 5th, 3rd)

Example 8a is an F#-7 bebop scale superimposed over a C major triad. The #11's (the F#, a common tone to both scales) of the C major scale are synchronized to fall on the first beat of each bar. However there is no "C" within the scale. A C# is synchronized with the 3rd beats of each bar. This being the case, **the scale can't be termed a C scale of any kind or type.** It can only be described as an F#-7 played **over** a C maj. Describing superimposed scales in this manner is awkward Naming conventions become difficult when trying to find a term for a superimposed musical idea. Whether the scale sounds "in" or "out" to you, it sounds "in" to me. As pianist Richie Beirach once said to me "Hal, it **all** sounds "in" to me." He had developed his hearing to the point where dissonances sounded consonant to him. In the above case the superimposed scale is independent of the chord symbol.

To build the case for superimposed melodies as being independent of the changes a short digression is in order.

There is a convention jazz improvisers use, to minimize the amount of scale and chord information they need to learn by reducing scales to their simplest form. Jazz pianist and educator Barry Harris reduces every scale to being one form or another of either a major or minor 6th scale. A more modern version that, for the lack of a better term, might be called "Scale Equivalents," is when all scales are reduced into one form or another of the four dominant 7th scales: (Dom 7th, Dom 7th #11, Dom 7th b9 (which also includes the diminished scale), and the Dom 7th augmented scale.

For example: The notes of the C7#11 scale also fit the notes to a D7b13, E-9b5, F#7 Alt., G-Maj.7, A7b9,#9,b13, and Bb Maj.7, Aug 5.

Example 9:

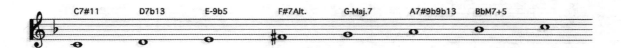

When played from root name to root name, with the appropriately named chord behind them, they each sound like the named scale, not a C7#11. When the root names are changed so are the chord tones of each Scale Equivalent. The chord tones of the D7b13, for example, will be still remain D, F#, A and C. When the four dominants are transposed into all twelve keys each chord type that exists in modern jazz nomenclature is listed once. Create a chart of these equivalents in all 12 keys and you'll notice that E-9b5 and A7 altered are the two dominant 7th #11 scales C7#11 (example 9) and Eb7#11 (example 10).

Example 10:

This results in now having two Dom 7th #11 scales that spell out E-9b5 and A7 Alt.

Taking an example of cell improvising from the preceding chapter we have the following cell pattern occurring on both scale equivalents.

Example 11:

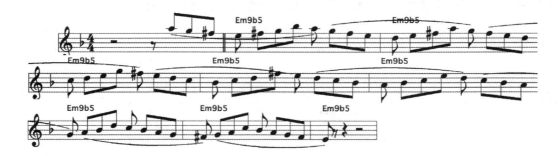

Example 12:

Any group on one scale can go to any group on the following scale.

Example 13:

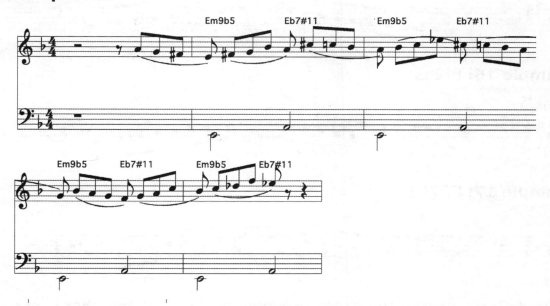

Again, naming conventions fall short of making accurate descriptions of the groupings in terms of the changes they are played over. The only way they can be successfully conceived is as groupings independent of the named chord change.

Returning to the concept of superimposed bebop scales as illustrated in example 8a, each of the scales in examples 9 & 10 can be played as bebop scales and superimposed of any of the scale's equivalents. Examples 14 – 19 are all on the C7#11 scale equivalent.

Example 14: C7#11

CHAPTER 9

Example 15: D7b13

Example 16: E-9b5

Example 17: F#7Alt

As with every rule there are exceptions. Some of the chord tones in the diatonic bebop Dom.#11 scales are "out of synch" with the "on" beats. In example 17, the added half-step could alternately be added between the "Bb" and the "C."

Example 18: G-Maj.7

Example 19: A7b9#9

In example 19 there is no third. If desired, the "C" natural can be substituted by a C#.

Example 20: BbMaj.7+5

In this example the added half-step was added between the "D" and the "E." It could also be added between the "E" and the "F#."

Applying the same process as in example 13, any bebop scale of a Dom7#11 can go to any scale of the next one.

Example 21:

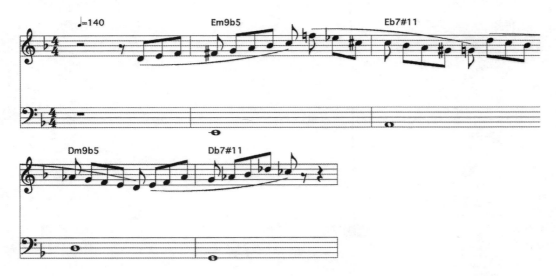

Explore the possible combinations of the groupings as in example 23 as well as those in example 21.

Superimposition is an advanced concept and as such, will be difficult to implement until you have achieved firm control over all basic tempos,

CHAPTER 9

scales and chord changes to the degree that you don't have to think about them. Only then can you apply superimposition to free yourself from the basics, achieving musical freedom.

HOW TO PRACTICE *FORWARD MOTION*

"Everything is a pick-up" – **Miles Davis**

The **process** you use to practice *Forward Motion* exercises is crucial to changing the way you hear. It's not only **what** you practice that is important, it's **how** you practice, **because, as a performance tool, you bring to the bandstand the <u>process itself</u>, not the musical ideas you practiced.**

Inner Processes

Practicing is external behavior that affects internal processes that in turn affects external behavior, i.e. performance. The three functions interact.

Practicing	Trained Internal Processes	Performance
External Behaviour →	Internal Behaviour →	External Behaviour

CHAPTER 10

Taking this idea to it's logical extreme, playing a musical instrument is, fundamentally, a process of "mind over matter."

"The imagination can manipulate ivory, felt, steel and spruce to sublime ends. Evans called it putting emotion into the piano and he proved that it can be done..." from BILL EVANS (Yale): How My Heart Sings By Peter Pettinger.

Most students give primary consideration to the external, technical and mechanical aspects of study: notation, theory, the instrument, mechanical technique, all those aspects of playing music that are visible to the naked eye. Your instrument, whichever one it may be, IS NOT THE INSTRUMENT. It just looks that way. The external aspects are an illusion.

In his article "*Can You Teach Musicality*," (May/June 1997 issue of *Piano & Keyboard magazine*) Seymour Fink states "By restricting our instruction to the teaching the mechanical (getting around and pushing the right levers) and teaching notation (lines, spaces, rhythmic subdivisions and the like), we ignore - or worse, might even obstruct - the true musical development of a student." He further suggests that "the essence of music making... Is found in inner hearing with its linkage to the body, and in a deeper grasp of musical values and their relationship to performance." "... Along with teaching notation, we must also teach its limitations, namely that it is an approximate, pictorially inadequate representation of those live and vital sounds that started in the composer's head. That music exists only in live sound, not on the page, is too quickly forgotten."

The musical realities are internal processes. The conclusion that follows may be difficult for the student to at first grasp: **YOU ARE THE INSTRUMENT.** A musical instrument is merely a machine. It is an input and output device. The mind, the body and emotions are the basic tools of any artistic endeavor. They can be trained to do the improviser's bidding.

The goals of practicing are to develop one's internal processes. The goal of playing is to use these processes as performance tools. An instrument, like the keyboard of a computer, is an input device used to train internal processes. When performing, an instrument acts like a computer's printer. It is the output device. The internal processes can be compared to software code that you're constantly writing and rewriting.

The internal life of an artist takes precedence over the external life. It is within this internal life that the richness of creative and controlled musical experience can be discovered, developed and enhanced. Being somewhat ephemeral in nature and initially difficult to grasp, this inner life is often ignored in favor of the external life. All practicing is dedicated to the development and control of inner processes.

CHAPTER 10

What Miles is suggesting is that every melodic line is a pick-up, is in motion towards the next melodic line. All the examples in FM start as a pick-up, outside the first bar line.

There are only three pickups. Most scale lines are combinations of three-note pick-ups, two-note pick-ups, and one-note pick-ups. (See examples # 4a, 4b, and 4c below). Improvisers mix these pick-ups to create interesting phrasing. Each of the pick-ups is heard differently in the ear. (Note the phrasing marks).

Example 1: (starts on beats "and" of three, "and" of one)

Example 2: (starts on beats four and two)

Example 3: (starts on beats "and" of four, "and" of two)

Note that this pick-up creates a duple feeling.

The notes on "one" and "three" of the bar are Target Notes. Before approaching a Target Note you must be able to hear it in advance.

Playing the target note first gives your ear the right information, a place for your ear to hear toward. You also need to give the ear something logical to work with.

Vivid Imagination and Focused Concentration

Students don't often have a clear understanding of the difference between practicing and performance and how the two interact. There is a practicing attitude and a playing attitude. Each attitude is different.

The Practicing Attitude

The main contributor to confusion between these two attitudes is that students spend more time practicing as compared to the amount of time spent playing. Without realizing it, they are developing a practicing attitude. Mistakenly, they try to apply this practicing attitude to a playing situation, becoming frustrated when it doesn't work. The main challenge most students face in developing a playing attitude is having the opportunity to gain enough playing experience with musicians of a high enough caliber to develop a playing attitude.

CHAPTER 10

The Playing Attitude

The playing attitude employs a process yet to be codified in western music education, "Faking It." Although the name has a slightly disreputable connotation, as if Faking It were somehow "cheating," it is a highly sophisticated process that can only be self-taught.

When studying music as a child, most of us share the common experience, (especially those with exceptional capacities for hearing), of our teachers discouraging us from memorizing and playing music by ear. Our early teachers implanted within us guilty feelings when we played by ear, as if it was wrong to do so.

Kochevitsky proved (see below) that all music is played by ear. That you can't play anything until you can hear it first. In scientific terms, developing a strong brain-to-hand signal. He also proved that if the signal from the brain is strong enough, the hands will do anything to get the sound out.

The process of Faking It is implemented by bringing these highly developed internal processes to the bandstand and just "going for it" without worrying about making a mistake. During a recent study by neurological researchers at the University of Tubingen, Germany, Dr. Gabriela Scheler, a former violinist with the Nuremberg Philharmonic Orchestra, said "the findings suggest that professionals have 'liberated' their minds from worrying about hitting the right notes. As a result, they are able to listen, judge and control their play..."

Learning how to Fake It can't be learned in the classroom and practice room. It can only be learned on the bandstand, doing it over and over, performance by performance, until you get it right. It's a process of experimentation and trial and error. The player is constantly trying to train and use these inner processes through the direct experience of using them.

My first experience with Faking It was during my early student years. I'd take commercial music gigs to make the rent, playing weddings, dances, Bar Mitzvah's. The tunes we played for these occasions were the classic standard songs. I didn't know enough of them to play them all by memory so I'd bring my fake books with me to the gigs. Unfortunately, the tunes segued from one to the next and the bandleaders never gave me enough time to look the tunes up. They'd usually say "Fake it kid, fake it. You'll learn it in a couple of choruses." By listening hard to the bass player, or if you were lucky, a guitar player, you'd eventually learn the tunes by ear.

Practicing is work directed toward developing internal processes. Playing is learned through direct experience, applying these internal processes until they work for you on the bandstand.

CHAPTER 10

INTERNAL PROCESSES

Historically, the practicing attitude is linear, intellectual, goal oriented and mechanical. The playing attitude is just the opposite. It is holistic, process oriented, and intuitive/emotional in nature.

Two of the internal processes that one must develop are a "vivid" aural imagination and the ability to concentrate in a highly focused and uninterrupted manner.

AURAL IMAGINATION

"First, learn how to hear everything and play everything you hear, then hear everything and play as little of it as possible"
(HG)

When I ask my class to raise their hands if they 're having trouble playing what they hear in their ears, for the most part, they all raise their hands. The truth is that they hear what they want to play but the don't hear it vividly, in an intense manner. They hear it pale as: Do-be-do-be-bop, instead of: **DO-BE-DO-BE-BOP**.

A TV documentary showed Dizzy backstage after a high school concert talking to some budding high school musicians. Trying to make his point about the degree to which vivid hearing must be developed, he sang the above scat syllables first softly "Do-be-do-be-bop" then very loudly, shouting "**DO-BE-DO-BE-BOP.**"

This brings up another concept that bears much contemplation to understand: **What's going on in your head comes out on your instrument on a direct one-to-one basis.** There's no hiding. Everybody plays exactly the way they hear. If you want to change the way you play you have to change the way your hear. You can't have an action without a thought that proceeds it. Conversely, all actions can be read backwards to understand a person's thought processes. To change one's actions, one must first change one's thought processes.

Kochevitsky's point about hearing was further confirmed by a later experience.

While touring with the Phil Woods band, I was in my motel room very early one morning, packing and getting ready to get into the van for a drive to our next gig. The TV was on to the morning kid's show *Mr. Rogers*. The great classical pianist Andre Watts was his guest. As I was on my way out the motel room door with suitcase in hand, I heard Mr. Rogers ask Andre " Well Andre, how do you play music?" I thought this a very interesting question and paused at the door to hear his response. He said " it all depends on the vividness of your imagination

CHAPTER 10

and how intensely you can concentrate." I was stunned as his answer was exactly the same as Kochevitsky's conclusions only stated in humanistic rather than scientific terms. What he means by imagination is "Aural" imagination. It depends on how intensely the aural signal is in the ear.

I had the good fortune to have studied piano technique with Madame Chaloff (jazz baritone saxophonist Serge Chaloff's mother) while living in Boston in the late 50's, early 60's. She used tell me "Hal, technique is in the brain, not in the hands." "Yeah, sure," I'd respond sarcastically, " then why are my hands so slow?" It wasn't until many years later, after my research on how the mind and nervous system work together that I finally became convinced of her argument. To prove her point to myself, I tried an experiment: Someone had sent me a bootleg Italian recording of air-checks that Art Tatum had made when he was in his early 20's. Tatum, being young and showing off, was playing the fastest piano I'd ever heard. I put the record on and listened to it for three hours straight. Immediately afterward I went to the piano and started playing. For about a half-hour I was playing as fast as Tatum. As I continued on for another half-hour my playing got slower and slower until I was back to my own technical level. What had happened was that by listening so long to Tatum playing fast, I had put the sound of playing fast in my ears. It was at that point that Madame Chaloff's point became a revelation; Tatum didn't have faster hands, he had faster ears. How fast you can play depends on how fast you can hear. Everyone has an upper limit of hearing speed that they work on extending over the years.

In another perfect example of the power of musical imagination, Oliver Sacks, in his article "*Prodigies*" (*The New Yorker Magazine*, Jan. 1995) sites the well-documented case of Blind Tom, a slave child born on a southern plantation in the mid 1800's. "Tom would listen intensely to the colonel's daughters practicing their sonatas and minuets on the piano." At four years old, when sat at the piano he'd repeat what they played note for note, at speed. Realizing this unique talent, he was subsequently sold to a promoter who took the child on tour. "At eleven, he played before President Buchanan at the White House. A panel of musicians who thought that he had tricked the President, tested his memory the following day, playing two entirely new compositions to him, thirteen and twenty pages in length; he reproduced them perfectly, and without the least apparent effort." The point here is how could he do that without any musical training? It is too easy to dismiss this as only another case of an idiot-savant. If we accept Kochevitsky's premise that all music is played by ear, then the only conclusion one can come to is that the child's aural imagination was extremely highly developed. This kind of hearing is commonplace among the great musicians.

CHAPTER 10

The ears (hearing) have their own independent way of working. They have their own dynamics and tendencies that can be used and manipulated to your advantage. Practicing and playing without understanding how the most basic tool of your art works is inefficient and largely nonproductive.

There is only one way you can play a musical idea...because you have to. The idea lives so intensely, so "vividly" in your aural (ears/hearing) imagination that you're compelled to play it. Your hands have no choice. They are compelled to respond to the intense brain signal. It is compulsive behavior in its finest form.

When practicing music ideas we tend think that it is the idea itself that we are trying to learn when in actuality the idea functions more as a tool to develop the more sophisticated process of vivid aural imagination. It's not the idea itself that is important, it is the effect that practicing the idea has on the process of hearing vividly. It is not the practiced idea you take to the bandstand with you, it is the process of vivid aural imagination you take to the bandstand as a performing tool. You don't want to improvise using only practiced ideas anyway. You'll find it extremely boring and mechanical. Your goal is get on the bandstand, make up ideas you never practiced before and hear them so intensely you are compelled to play them.

Man's imagination is the most powerful tool in the universe. It is the source of all civilization. For example:

Someone, sometime in the far past, decided they were tired of sitting on cold, hard rocks and wondered if there was a better alternative they could come up with The concept of the chair was invented. The inventor tried to first imagine what a chair would look like and imagined a two-legged chair. After getting black and blue from falling off the thing, the inventor imagined that adding another leg to it might make it more stable, and it did. Seeking increased stability, the inventor further imagined adding a fourth and then a fifth leg, through trial and error concluding that four legs did the job. At each stage, from conception to realization, an overall goal was imagined followed by imagining the incremental steps to achieve it.

Nothing created by mankind exists without it being first imagined. Some eastern religions even go so far as to postulate that the observable universe is actually a product of our imaginations. No matter the art form, harnessing the power of your imagination and concentration are what being an artist is all about.

Chapter 10

CONCENTRATION

Without realizing it, people switch mental states thousands of times a day. One minute you'll be aware of everything going on around you, the next minute you'll switch to an introspective, self-absorbed state. Sometimes you have to concentrate on more than one thing at a time, as a juggler would have to do. Mental states can be eventually controlled and mastered as tools of your art. Concentration is a mental state and is hard work.

"Work," in the human organism, is measured by the amount of calories burned during a task. A scientific study compared the amount of calories burned by someone digging a ditch for eight hours to that of a classical cellist playing a three-hour concert. <u>They both burned the same amount of calories</u> yet all the cellist was doing was sitting and moving a bow back and forth. The ditch digger's work was physical. The cellist's was concentration. Concentration is the "work" we do as performers. You've had the experience of having practiced very intensely for an hour or two and finding yourself exhausted afterward. There's no denying it. It's work.

Unawares, we are developing concentration when we practice. Not only does a practiced idea shape one's hearing, it also improves your ability to concentrate. This ability, like vivid imagining, may take years to develop. Concentration comes in many forms: narrow, wide, divided, and distracted. Exercising control over these types of concentration and using them as tools is another of your goals. One in particular is narrow concentration. Narrow concentration focuses on a narrow point, as in meditation. How many times, while playing, has your mind drifted off to think about what your old lady said to you earlier that day? Or what your dog did that afternoon? Your flow of concentration is interrupted. You can concentrate, but only in spurts. What remains to be developed is the ability to concentrate in a continuous uninterrupted flow.

When practicing a particular musical idea, we are focused narrowly on the idea, focusing in a manner excludes all extraneous thoughts. Our general awareness of things around us recedes until the idea is the only thing we are aware of, becoming almost all consuming. In that way we are, without realizing it, practicing narrow concentration.

This refers again to the subject of "work" and what kind of "work" we do as performers. The reader may never have been told this: playing music is supposed to be easy. Most of us think it's supposed to be hard to play, but truthfully, you can't play music well if it's hard to do. If you can't do it easily you can't have fun and project that feeling of fun to your band-mates and listeners. Anything you can do to make the music easier to play is okay. It's not, as often believed, cheating to make it easier.

CHAPTER 10

Most students physically over-work when they play. I have, in my private teaching, quite effectively turned these students on to distracted concentration by having a conversation with them while playing together.

I discovered distracted concentration one evening when I was playing a steady solo piano gig at a restaurant in a Boston suburb.

There was no bandstand and the piano was on the same level as the restaurant's tables, which, unfortunately, made it easier for customers to come to the piano to make requests. One evening a blue-haired old lady came up to the piano and started talking to me while I was in the middle of a solo portion of some tune. I didn't stop soloing while we talked. As the discussion progressed I started to notice that I was improvising ideas I had never played before. I was knocked out. I kept saying to myself "Gee, I didn't know I knew that lick," or "Wow, I didn't know I could play this." It was all new stuff to me and it was coming out so easy, without trying. By taking my mental focus off my playing, I allowed my intuition and subconscious to take over the soloing, accessing a more creative inner resource.

Correcting Outmoded Practice Habits

Most musicians started playing music during childhood. Learning, at this stage, is achieved through the process of unremitting repetition, an appropriate process for that stage of musical development. The goals of childhood and adult practicing differ. Consequently, the processes involved in achieving these goals should differ as well.

As a child we have no choice as to how and what to practice. Our early teachers were authoritarian. They told us what to do. Adults have the ability to chose, to make their own decisions, thereby exerting control over their practicing habits. There are a number of tacit conditioning habits created during childhood that, unawares, is carried over into adult practicing. One of them is repetition and its attendant problems. Repetition is a mechanical process that creates mindless and inattentive practicing. Improvisation is a creative process. Using a mechanical process to learn a creative process is non-productive. Mechanicalism doesn't develop the ability to concentrate in a focused manner. It also doesn't promote "Vivid Imagination."

As a creative musician you must have wondered, at one time or another, at how musical ideas are imparted with "meaning." How a musical idea is brought forward from the inner depths of a person's

CHAPTER 10

mind, through the machine we call a musical instrument out from that machine, through the air to affect a listener emotionally. It is through the process called "Vivid Imagining" and "Focused Concentration." These are **the basic tools of any creative artist** no matter the artistic medium and are the tools you need to develop.

Correcting old habits will be a constant battle until you reestablish adult practicing habits to the point they become as automatic as your tendency to mindlessly repeat. Your goal is to practice everything with "meaning" so you can play "meaningful" music. Practicing using Vivid Imagining and Focused Concentration is the way to reach this goal. Focused Concentration is built in to the Vivid Imagining technique.

Musical ideas are played because they exist so intensely in your musical imagination that you have no choice but to play them. Practicing using Vivid Imagining involves a step by step process that eventually increases the intensity of everything you hear. It is very similar to programming your thinking and is comprised of two stages: Preparation and Execution. Use this technique for everything you practice.

PREPARATION

1. Always practice with a tape recorder on. When I'm teaching this technique in a one-to-one private lesson I can tell by the way the musical idea was played whether it was vividly imagined by the amount of feeling (not volume) given to the idea. Vividly played ideas have a singable quality. Because of this the note's tone projects, taking on the aspect of a singing tone. It may take a while to learn the difference between an idea played with feeling and one that is not. The difference may seem subtle to you but it makes all the difference in the world to the listener.

2. Put your hands on your instrument and keep them there. Don't let too much time to pass between preparing to play the idea and its execution. You could lose the immediate affect of the programming. If you play a wind instrument keep the mouthpiece in your mouth. If a pianist or guitarist, keep your hands on the keyboard or fret board. Put your finger(s) over what would be the first note of your exercise. Soundlessly pre-rehearse the exercise's fingerings

3. In your mind, YELL the inner guide-tone melody as loud as you can, at the tempo you want to play it (the top speed at which can play an idea will be your upper limit to hearing fast. Over time that upper limit will increase), nailing the intonation. Yell it so loud that you're aware of nothing else but the sound of the idea in your head. If it's a long musical idea you may want to break the idea into smaller segments, incrementally adding the segments together. Play each segment separately, then join two segments together to see if you can hear the duration of both ideas.

CHAPTER 10

Add the third segment. When adding segments always start from the first idea. The goal is to extend and sustain vivid imagination over longer and longer periods.

EXECUTION

Immediately after preparing the idea, offhandedly "toss" the idea off without trying. Just let it happen. If your ear is properly programmed it will do the work for you. Not trying will probably be the most difficult aspect of the process. We are all brought up having been conditioned to "try" when working to achieve a goal. This is good and proper education for every-day goal orientation. However, there is a kind of "trying" artist's employ that is not like the every-day type. It is a trying without trying. More of a "letting" than a trying. Watch a painter working with a brush. Their hands will hold the brush very lightly so that the strokes look almost undirected. They're letting their training do the work. It's kind of Zen a thing in that you're not going to get it until you stop trying to get it. The harder you try the further away you get from it. You have to build trust in your training and instincts. Most lack this trust and to compensate, using every-day trying.

4. If you make a mistake, return to step number one again. Your immediate impulse will be to repeat the idea again without going through the process. Resist that impulse.

5. The steps between Preparation and Execution should follow each other as quickly as possible. If too much time lapses between steps your ear could lose the previous programming.

In the next example (#4), notice that the Target Notes (on 1 & 3) are, in themselves, consecutive ascending and descending scale tones. The Target Notes move in a manner you are familiar with, in a logical progression. You get a clear and logical idea of where your scale's going (your series of Target Notes) since each succeeding last note is a scale step higher or lower than the preceding one. **Always play the target notes first and in tempo.** Every melody has a target note. Before mindlessly repeating a musical idea, define its Inner Guide Tone Melody. Practice this first.

Play the series of target notes (the ascending scale line) to place them in your ear, then try to approach each Target Note from one scale tone above. The Target Notes themselves are the Inner Guide Tone Melody. Your ear may "run out" of hearing in FM half way through the exercises. If so, start simpler. Play the first Target Note, at the same time singing it in your head (not out loud.), then approach it from one scale tone above. Do the same for each succeeding scale tone. Once you can do this, play the Target Note Melody, while singing it your head, then see if you can play all the approaches and their target notes in tempo, without stopping or pausing.

CHAPTER 10

If you make a mistake in any of these exercises, don't repeat the phrase thoughtlessly. The exercise itself is important but the process of playing the last note first, giving your ear a place to go toward, is the most important aspect of all. Putting the target note in your ear will let your ear work for you. Without thinking about it, the ear will carry the approach to it. **Play these exercises in strict tempo.**

Confirm you're are hearing ahead by taping yourself while practicing. One of the tests that will tell you you're not playing in FM yet is a tendency to still accent the first note of an Approach, even if it is on an up beat. This habit is learned from always starting melodies on the first beat of the bar which has a natural built-in emphasis. This tendency to emphasize first notes can carry over into your FM practicing. If you're still accenting the first note, you're not hearing ahead. The last note, on 1 & 3, should have the emphasis. If you're still emphasizing the first note try putting the emphasis on the target note. It will then have a tendency to loom in the future as a target point. Once you've corrected the first note emphasis, play the groupings smoothly, totally devoid of accents, so they sound like one long line rather than separate groupings strung together.

Another habit that shows you're not hearing ahead is pausing before you hit the Target Note. That shows that the Target Note is not in your ear as a place to go toward.

Don't play these exercises using your intellectual memory. Play them by ear, using your auditory memory. Select your exercise and play it without looking at the paper. This forces you to use your ear.

Example 4: a half a beat ahead

Example 5: a whole beat ahead

CHAPTER 10

Example 6: a beat and a half ahead

Adjust the octaves when range becomes a problem.

If, as in the example above, you have difficulty in hearing the interval between the Target Note and the first note of the next approach, it's because the sound of the interval is not in your ear. This interval is the "Connector" interval, the distance between the last note of one idea and the first note of the next is often hard to hear. Overcome this difficulty (or any other) by making a separate exercise out of the pairs of last and first notes (the connector intervals in Example 6) as they ascend or descend the scale. For example:

Example 7:

Last 1st.   Last 1st.

Notice that the intervals are scale fifths and root-5th of the diatonic 7th chords in the key of C. Play this exercise until you can hear their melodic content then go back to the original exercise to see if you can play it without pausing.

Example 8: two beats ahead

At this point the exercises become longer. You should have the idea by now and be able to play the exercises with descending target notes, as in the preceding examples.

Example 9: Two and a half beats ahead

CHAPTER 10

Examine the following exercises closely. You'll notice that they are now combinations of the preceding ones. As the scale exercises lengthen, each phrase will contain two target notes forming an Inner Guide Tone Melody that will guide you through the exercise.

Example 10:

Example 11: three beats ahead

Example 12: three & a half beats ahead

In Example 12 you're now playing the complete scale for a full octave. Practice these exercises in all twelve keys. The other keys will be easier to play because of the work you have done with the previous exercises.

Experiment combining various Melodic Inversions approaching different target notes from above and below.

Try starting at any note in a scale, and any beat in the bar, to see if you can hear your line approaching and resolving on "1" and/or "3" of the bars.

If you'd like to see how the great improvisers use *Forward Motion* in their playing, take any transcribed solo and circle the notes that fall on "1" & "3" of the bar. For an even more accurate analysis, circle the notes at the beginning of each quarter-note.

All practicing is ear training of one sort or another. The question is

CHAPTER 10

then, are you training your ears to work properly? Is your practice time being used in its most efficient manner?

Music publications commonly write their scale exercises without *Forward Motion*. They start on "one" of the bar and on the root of a scale, which, is the strongest note in the scale and is, therefore, according to FM Theory, the last note of the scale, not the first. Because it's the strongest beat of the bar, it's the safest, most secure beat of the bar to start ideas on. Getting used to starting melodies on off beats will feel insecure at first. However, when the ear is fed the information it requires to function naturally, the ear does the work for you and carries your line to its resolution.

Musical ideas, if they don't make sense to the ear, if they're not being played logically, are harder to learn. The ear gravitates toward logical (strong) musical ideas, retains them quicker and tends to reject ideas that are weak (chaotic).

The ear has it's own dynamic. Once practicing FM has begun you can't go back to your earlier way of hearing because the ear wants to hear this way. Music won't sound the same way to you as it did before, especially your own playing. Until you've changed your playing around to FM it will sound worse to you than it did before because now you'll be hearing in a natural manner.

Most students become depressed when first learning how to play in FM. Their playing sounds worse to them. This is not, however, an unhappy occasion, it is positive. It means that you are now hearing mistakes in your playing you'd never heard before. Your hearing has become more sophisticated. You'll also notice that you're hearing other's playing differently as well. Jazz is a music that is based on learning by listening to the music 28 hours a day. If you're not hearing it correctly, you're not learning it correctly.

Organizing Your Practive

One of the perennial questions students ask me is how to organize their practicing when coping with huge amounts of new information. When I was a new student at Berklee School of Music in the mid 1950's, I was inundated with massive amounts of new information. So much so my head was spinning. I was eventually forced into developing my own methodology for organizing this. Comparing my system to others I found that each musician had developed their own practicing methodology. From this comparison it became clear to me that there were as many ways of organizing ones practicing as there were persons organizing it. In other words, in the end, each musician has to develop their own

CHAPTER 10

individual methodology according the way their mind works. The way you organize your practicing will have a direct influence on your future style of playing. Borrowing another musician's practicing regimen may initially help you get your practicing organized but in the end we are all left up to our own devices to figure out our own way to absorb new information. The sooner one develops their individual practicing regimen the better, as it will be a process you'll use for the rest of your life. The goals of organizing your practice are efficiency, logic, and thoroughness.

The theories in *Forward Motion* are presented in a way that was shaped by my individually developed methodology. Take the information herein and find your own way to develop it.

SHER MUSIC CO. — *The finest in Jazz & Latin Publications*

THE NEW REAL BOOK SERIES

The Standards Real Book (C, Bb or Eb)

A Beautiful Friendship
A Time For Love
Ain't No Sunshine
Alice In Wonderland
All Of You
Alone Together
At Last
Baltimore Oriole
Bess, You Is My Woman
Bluesette
But Not For Me
Close Enough For Love
Crazy He Calls Me
Dancing In The Dark

Days Of Wine And Roses
Dreamsville
Easy To Love
Embraceable You
Falling In Love With Love
From This Moment On
Give Me The Simple Life
Have You Met Miss Jones?
Hey There
I Can't Get Started
I Concentrate On You
I Cover The Waterfront
I Love You
I Loves You Porgy

I Only Have Eyes For You
I'm A Fool To Want You
Indian Summer
It Ain't Necessarily So
It Never Entered My Mind
It's You Or No One
Just One Of Those Things
Love For Sale
Lover, Come Back To Me
The Man I Love
Mr. Lucky
My Funny Valentine
My Heart Stood Still
My Man's Gone Now

Old Folks
On A Clear Day
Our Love Is Here To Stay
'Round Midnight
Secret Love
September In The Rain
Serenade In Blue
Shiny Stockings
Since I Fell For You
So In Love
So Nice (Summer Samba)
Some Other Time
Stormy Weather
The Summer Knows

Summer Night
Summertime
Teach Me Tonight
That Sunday, That Summer
The Girl From Ipanema
Then I'll Be Tired Of You
There's No You
Time On My Hands
'Tis Autumn
Where Or When
Who Cares?
With A Song In My Heart
You Go To My Head
And Hundreds More!

The New Real Book - Volume 1 (C, Bb or Eb)

Angel Eyes
Anthropology
Autumn Leaves
Beautiful Love
Bernie's Tune
Blue Bossa
Blue Daniel
But Beautiful
Chain Of Fools
Chelsea Bridge
Compared To What
Darn That Dream
Desafinado
Early Autumn

Eighty One
E.S.P.
Everything Happens To Me
Feel Like Makin' Love
Footprints
Four
Four On Six
Gee Baby Ain't I Good
To You
Gone With The Wind
Here's That Rainy Day
I Love Lucy
I Mean You
I Should Care

I Thought About You
If I Were A Bell
Imagination
The Island
Jersey Bounce
Joshua
Lady Bird
Like Someone In Love
Little Sunflower
Lush Life
Mercy, Mercy, Mercy
The Midnight Sun
Monk's Mood
Moonlight In Vermont

My Shining Hour
Nature Boy
Nefertiti
Nothing Personal
Oleo
Once I Loved
Out Of This World
Pent Up House
Portrait Of Tracy
Put It Where You Want It
Robbin's Nest
Ruby, My Dear
Satin Doll
Search For Peace

Shaker Song
Skylark
A Sleepin' Bee
Solar
Speak No Evil
St. Thomas
Street Life
Tenderly
These Foolish Things
This Masquerade
Three Views Of A Secret
Waltz For Debby
Willow Weep For Me
And Many More!

The New Real Book Play-Along CDs (For Volume 1)

CD #1 - Jazz Classics - Lady Bird, Bouncin' With Bud, Up Jumped Spring, Monk's Mood, Doors, Very Early, Eighty One, Voyage **& More!**
CD #2 - Choice Standards - Beautiful Love, Darn That Dream, Moonlight In Vermont, Trieste, My Shining Hour, I Should Care **& More!**
CD #3 - Pop-Fusion - Morning Dance, Nothing Personal, La Samba, Hideaway, This Masquerade, Three Views Of A Secret, Rio **& More!**
World-Class Rhythm Sections, featuring Mark Levine, Larry Dunlap, Sky Evergreen, Bob Magnusson, Keith Jones, Vince Lateano & Tom Hayashi

The New Real Book - Volume 2 (C, Bb or Eb)

Afro-Centric
After You've Gone
Along Came Betty
Bessie's Blues
Black Coffee
Blues For Alice
Body And Soul
Bolivia
The Boy Next Door
Bye Bye Blackbird
Cherokee
A Child Is Born
Cold Duck Time
Day By Day

Django
Equinox
Exactly Like You
Falling Grace
Five Hundred Miles High
Freedom Jazz Dance
Giant Steps
Harlem Nocturne
Hi-Fly
Honeysuckle Rose
I Hadn't Anyone 'Til You
I'll Be Around
I'll Get By
Ill Wind

I'm Glad There Is You
Impressions
In Your Own Sweet Way
It's The Talk Of The Town
Jordu
Killer Joe
Lullaby Of The Leaves
Manha De Carneval
The Masquerade Is Over
Memories Of You
Moment's Notice
Mood Indigo
My Ship
Naima

Nica's Dream
Once In A While
Perdido
Rosetta
Sea Journey
Senor Blues
September Song
Seven Steps To Heaven
Silver's Serenade
So Many Stars
Some Other Blues
Song For My Father
Sophisticated Lady
Spain

Stablemates
Stardust
Sweet And Lovely
That's All
There Is No Greater Love
'Til There Was You
Time Remembered
Turn Out The Stars
Unforgettable
While We're Young
Whisper Not
Will You Still Be Mine?
You're Everything
And Many More!

The New Real Book - Volume 3 (C, Bb, Eb or Bass clef)

Actual Proof
Ain't That Peculiar
Almost Like Being In Love
Another Star
Autumn Serenade
Bird Of Beauty
Black Nile
Blue Moon
Butterfly
Caravan
Ceora
Close Your Eyes
Creepin'
Day Dream

Dolphin Dance
Don't Be That Way
Don't Blame Me
Emily
Everything I Have Is Yours
For All We Know
Freedomland
The Gentle Rain
Get Ready
A Ghost Of A Chance
Heat Wave
How Sweet It Is
I Fall In Love Too Easily
I Got It Bad

I Hear A Rhapsody
If You Could See Me Now
In A Mellow Tone
In A Sentimental Mood
Inner Urge
Invitation
The Jitterbug Waltz
Just Friends
Just You, Just Me
Knock On Wood
The Lamp Is Low
Laura
Let's Stay Together
Lonely Woman

Maiden Voyage
Moon And Sand
Moonglow
My Girl
On Green Dolphin Street
Over The Rainbow
Prelude To A Kiss
Respect
Ruby
The Second Time Around
Serenata
The Shadow Of Your Smile
So Near, So Far
Solitude

Speak Like A Child
Spring Is Here
Stairway To The Stars
Star Eyes
Stars Fell On Alabama
Stompin' At The Savoy
Sweet Lorraine
Taking A Chance On Love
This Is New
Too High
(Used To Be A) Cha Cha
When Lights Are Low
You Must Believe In Spring
And Many More!

The All Jazz Real Book

Over 540 pages of tunes as recorded by:
Miles, Trane, Bill Evans, Cannonball, Scofield, Brecker, Yellowjackets, Bird, Mulgrew Miller, Kenny Werner, MJQ, McCoy Tyner, Kurt Elling, Brad Mehldau, Don Grolnick, Kenny Garrett, Patitucci, Jerry Bergonzi, Stanley Clarke, Tom Harrell, Herbie Hancock, Horace Silver, Stan Getz, Sonny Rollins, and MORE!

Includes a free CD of many of the melodies
(featuring Bob Sheppard & Friends.). $44 list price.
Available in C, Bb, Eb

The European Real Book

An amazing collection of some of the greatest jazz compositions ever recorded! Available in C, Bb and Eb. $40

- Over 100 of Europe's best jazz writers.
- 100% accurate, composer-approved charts.
- 400 pages of fresh, exciting sounds from virtually every country in Europe.
- Sher Music's superior legibility and signature calligraphy makes reading the music easy.

Listen to FREE MP3 FILES of many of the songs at **www.shermusic.com!**

LATIN MUSIC BOOKS, CDs, DVD

The Latin Real Book (C, Bb or Eb)

The only professional-level Latin fake book ever published!
Over 570 pages. Detailed transcriptions exactly as recorded by:

Ray Barretto	Arsenio Rodriguez	Manny Oquendo	Ivan Lins
Eddie Palmieri	Tito Rodriguez	Puerto Rico All-Stars	Djavan
Fania All-Stars	Orquesta Aragon	Issac Delgaldo	Tom Jobim
Tito Puente	Beny Moré	Ft. Apache Band	Toninho Horta
Ruben Blades	Cal Tjader	Dave Valentin	Joao Bosco
Los Van Van	Andy Narell	Paquito D'Rivera	Milton Nascimento
NG La Banda	Mario Bauza	Clare Fischer	Leila Pinheiro
Irakere	Dizzy Gilllespie	Chick Corea	Gal Costa
Celia Cruz	Mongo Santamaria	Sergio Mendes	**And Many More!**

The Latin Real Book Sampler CD

12 of the greatest Latin Real Book tunes as played by the original artists: Tito Puente, Ray Barretto, Andy Narell, Puerto Rico Allstars, Bacacoto, etc.

$16 list price. Available in U.S.A. only.

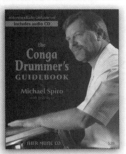

The Conga Drummer's Guidebook By Michael Spiro

Includes CD - $28 list price. The only method book specifically designed for the intermediate to advanced conga drummer. It goes behind the superficial licks and explains how to approach any Afro-Latin rhythm with the right feel, so you can create a groove like the pros!.

"This book is awesome. Michael is completely knowledgable about his subject."
– Dave Garibaldi

"A breakthrough book for all students of the conga drum."
– Karl Perazzo

Introduction to the Conga Drum - DVD
By Michael Spiro

For beginners, or anyone needing a solid foundation in conga drum technique.

Jorge Alabe – "Mike Spiro is a great conga teacher. People can learn real conga technique from this DVD."

John Santos – "A great musician/teacher who's earned his stripes"

1 hour, 55 minutes running time. $25.

Muy Caliente!

Afro-Cuban Play-Along CD and Book
Rebeca Mauleón - Keyboard
Oscar Stagnaro - Bass
Orestes Vilató - Timbales
Carlos Caro - Bongos
Edgardo Cambon - Congas
Over 70 min. of smokin' Latin grooves!
Stereo separation so you can eliminate the bass or piano. Play-along with a rhythm section featuring some of the top Afro-Cuban musicians in the world! $18.

The True Cuban Bass

By Carlos Del Puerto, (bassist with Irakere) and **Silvio Vergara**, $22.

For acoustic or electric bass; English and Spanish text; Includes CDs of either historic Cuban recordings or Carlos playing each exercise; Many transcriptions of complete bass parts for tunes in different Cuban styles – the roots of Salsa.

101 Montunos

By Rebeca Mauleón

The only comprehensive study of Latin piano playing ever published.

- Bi-lingual text (English/Spanish)
- 2 CDs of the author demonstrating each montuno
- Covers over 100 years of Afro-Cuban styles, including the danzón, guaracha, mambo, merengue and songo—from Peruchin to Eddie Palmieri. $28

The Salsa Guide Book

By Rebeca Mauleón

The only complete method book on salsa ever published! 260 pages. $25.

Carlos Santana – "A true treasure of knowledge and information about Afro-Cuban music."

Mark Levine, author of The Jazz Piano Book. – "This is the book on salsa."

Sonny Bravo, pianist with Tito Puente – "This will be the salsa 'bible' for years to come."

Oscar Hernández, pianist with Rubén Blades – "An excellent and much needed resource."

The Brazilian Guitar Book

By Nelson Faria, one of Brazil's best new guitarists.

- Over 140 pages of comping patterns, transcriptions and chord melodies for samba, bossa, baião, etc.
- Complete chord voicings written out for each example.
- Comes with a CD of Nelson playing each example.
- The most complete Brazilian guitar method ever published! $28.

Joe Diorio – "Nelson Faria's book is a welcome addition to the guitar literature. I'm sure those who work with this volume wiill benefit greatly"

Inside The Brazilian Rhythm Section

By Nelson Faria and Cliff Korman

This is the first book/CD package ever published that provides an opportunity for bassists, guitarists, pianists and drummers to interact and play-along with a master Brazilian rhythm section. Perfect for practicing both accompanying and soloing.

$28 list price for book and 2 CDs - including the charts for the CD tracks and sample parts for each instrument, transcribed from the recording.

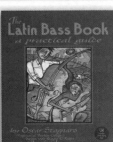

The Latin Bass Book
A PRACTICAL GUIDE
By Oscar Stagnaro

The only comprehensive book ever published on how to play bass in authentic Afro-Cuban, Brazilian, Caribbean, Latin Jazz & South American styles. $34.

Over 250 pages of transcriptions of Oscar Stagnaro playing each exercise. Learn from the best!

Includes: 3 Play-Along CDs to accompany each exercise, featuring world-class rhythm sections.

Afro-Caribbean Grooves for Drumset

By Jean-Philippe Fanfant, drummer with Andy narell's band, Sakesho.

Covers grooves from 10 Caribbean nations, arranged for drumset.

Endorsed by Peter Erskine, Horacio Hernandez, etc.

CD includes both audio and video files. $25.

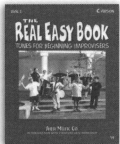

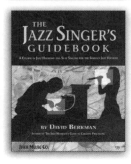